Christiane Katharina Murr

Beyond Green Marketing

Christiane Katharina Murr

Beyond Green Marketing

New Approaches for a possible Implementation of Sustainability in Marketing

VDM Verlag Dr. Müller

Imprint

Bibliographic information by the German National Library: The German National Library lists this publication at the German National Bibliography; detailed bibliographic information is available on the Internet at http://dnb.d-nb.de.

Any brand names and product names mentioned in this book are subject to trademark, brand or patent protection and are trademarks or registered trademarks of their respective holders. The use of brand names, product names, common names, trade names, product descriptions etc. even without a particular marking in this works is in no way to be construed to mean that such names may be regarded as unrestricted in respect of trademark and brand protection legislation and could thus be used by anyone.

Cover image: www.purestockx.com

Publisher:
VDM Verlag Dr. Müller Aktiengesellschaft & Co. KG, Dudweiler Landstr. 125 a, 66123 Saarbrücken, Germany,
Phone +49 681 9100-698, Fax +49 681 9100-988,
Email: info@vdm-verlag.de

Copyright © 2008 VDM Verlag Dr. Müller Aktiengesellschaft & Co. KG and licensors
All rights reserved. Saarbrücken 2008

Produced in USA and UK by:
Lightning Source Inc., La Vergne, Tennessee, USA
Lightning Source UK Ltd., Milton Keynes, UK
BookSurge LLC, 5341 Dorchester Road, Suite 16, North Charleston, SC 29418, USA

ISBN: 978-3-8364-8726-9

Table of Content

1 Introduction 1
2 Basics and explanations 2
  2.1 The pathway to sustainable development 2
  2.2 Sustainable development 4
  2.3 Marketing and sustainability 6
3 Awareness and behaviour 9
  3.1 Attempt to define sustainable oriented consumption 10
  3.2 General mood of consumers 11
  3.3 Purchase criteria 13
  3.4 Typology of consumers 15
  3.5 Retail and competition behaviour 17
4 Markets 20
  4.1 Market participants 21
  4.2 Challenges 23
  4.3 Industries 25
5 Environmental aware and social responsible business 30
  5.1 Motivations 32
  5.2 Implementation of sustainability 34
    5.2.1 Sustainability as corporate approach 35
    5.2.2 Sustainability in the organisational structure 37
  5.3 Communication 40
6 Formulation of strategic marketing in relation to sustainability 43
  6.1 Business types 43
  6.2 Sustainable oriented competitive strategies 45
  6.3 Planning instruments of strategic marketing 48
7 Instruments of marketing 51
  7.1 Product political measures 51
    7.1.1 Product responsibility 53
    7.1.2 Analysis 54
    7.1.3 Packaging policy 56
    7.1.4 Brand policy 58
  7.2 Communication policy 60
    7.2.1 Advertising 62
    7.2.2 Public Relations 66
    7.2.3 Labelling 68
    7.2.4 Sponsoring 70
  7.3 Price policy 72
  7.4 Distribution 75
8 Conclusion and outlook 78

List of literature

Appendix

Table of lists and figures

Table 2-1: Historic outlook 3
Table 2-2: Sustainability Check... 6
Figure 2-2: Areas of sustainable oriented marketing... 9

Table 3-1: Environmental attitudes of consumers 12
Figure 3-1: Customer typology 15
Figure 3-2: Dimensions of an ecological oriented competitive analysis 19
Figure 3-3: Competitive movers in apparel retail industry 19

Table 4-1: Example of a situational analysis in marketing 22
Figure 4-1: Sustainable affectedness of various industry 26

Figure 5-1: Environmental and social management system at Otto 38
Figure 5-2: Product Responsibility at Henkel 39

Table 6-1: Sustainable competitive strategies 47
Figure 6-1: Example for an impact/profitability portfolio 49
Figure 6-2: Example for an impact/customer value portfolio 50
Figure 6-3: Sustainable portfolio for products 50
Figure 6-4: Twodimensional sustainable portfolio 50

Figure 7-1: Typology of advertising in print media 64
Figure 7-2: Conflict potentials between retail and manufacturers 77

1 Introduction

In the past few years many products have been introduced on markets with additions 'eco' or 'organic'. These products seem to become even more environmental friendly and many corporations meanwhile confess to sound exposure to nature and responsible acting towards society. In economy a turnaround becomes apparent. The topic of sustainable development is not anymore important for a small group with corresponding environmental background, the rising orientation of consumers towards environmental and social acceptable problem solving made the topic important for industry and economy. It is now questioned if this trend reversal involves as well a measurable success for nature (e.g. greenhouse effect, energy consumption) and for human beings (e.g. child work, discrimination) or if it will ebb away in the endeavour of economic success.

Hereunto the German minister for environment *Sigmar Gabriel* expressed impressively: "future generations and a growing world population provoke challenges. Among others the increase of needs and the corresponding growth of markets behold chances for sustainability. Thereby suppressing of needs is no solution. Moreover needs should be satisfied in an environmental and social acceptable way. Instead of hindering markets and their growth, markets need to be shaped ecological and sustainable oriented. The counterproductive fight of markets against environment must become to a fight of markets for environment."[1]

Complementary the Chief Executive Officer of the chemical business *Degussa AG* Dr. *Klaus Engel* states that "pure economy is as short-sighted as pure ecology. A new kind of sustainable thinking has to establish: innovations and new technologies throughout the life cycle need to be focussed on introducing new sustainable product variants. Furthermore responsible behaviour in ecological concerns and social commitment is indispensable for the success of a global acting business."[2]

Sustainable behaviour in manufacturing and in consuming provokes at the same time economic and social advantages. The introduction and the maintenance of an authentic sustainable oriented tenor of the corporation should be regarded as a

---
[1] Cp. *Gabriel, Sigmar*, Innovation für Wirtschaft und Umwelt, Leitmärkte der Zukunft ökologisch erobern, BMU-Innovationskonferenz, dbb Forum Berlin, 30.10.2006
[2] Cp. *Schaltegger, Stefan,* in: Nachhaltiges Wirtschaften, Handelsblatt, 12. Juni 2006

market opportunity in which stakeholder relations especially to customers and markets can be improved as well as the image in public. For implementation each business has to define the concept of sustainable development for itself and set up an overall strategy; hereby marketing plays a key role.

In line proactive marketing encourages innovation and development of products respectively services. It influences and changes consumers' attitudes respectively consumption patterns as well as it communicates the corporations' differentness. Because it creates competitive advantage, marketing should not only orientate on an open communication policy. Moreover the emphasized sustainable arguments should be in line with the corporate concept of all marketing instruments.

In the following I am going to address the issue of corporations' possibilities to contribute to socio-ecological problems and thereby discuss variations of existing ecological orientated marketing instruments in respect to sustainability.

2 Basics and explanations

The subsequent chapter outlines the development of environmental protection and its involvement in managerial processes. Based on a short historic outline of environmental milestones the fundamental term sustainability is pointed out. In line with the success of sustainable development it is analysed how the concept can be marketed.

2.1 The pathway to sustainable development

In the past nature was categorised as inexhaustible potential. Thereby the complexity of the overall eco system was mostly ignored. Our established industrial system needs to be understood as part of the complete ecological system. We can only exist and our industrial system only functions in future if we are able to balance the ecological system. The publications of the *Club of Rome* can be regarded as cornerstone of the environmental movement. Other milestones which influenced the development are named in the following:[3]

---

[3] Cp. *Englfried, Justus*, Nachhaltiges Umweltmanagement, Oldenbourg Wissenschaftsverlag GmbH, München, 2004, p. 6 et seqq.

Table 2-1: Historic outlook

1974	The German Federal Immission control statute claims to introduce in companies a representative for immission control.
End of 1970ies	First comprehensive publications regarding environmental management.
Mid of 1980	The economy starts being proactive on environmental affairs and end of pipe technologies begin to emerge.
1987	The Brundtland Commission publishes its report 'Our Common Future' and therein calls on business to incorporate sustainable development.
1987	The International Chamber of Commerce develops a scheme for Environmental Auditing.
1989	The Federal Ministry for Environment publishes first results concerning the intention for environmental oriented management.
Beginning 1990	Emerging of the eco-balance movement.
1992	The United Nations Conference of Environment and Development (UNCEP) presents the Agenda 21 and provides a first approach for sustainable development.
1992	Great Britain installs as first European country a national norm for 'Environmental Management Systems' (BS 7750).
1993	Commencement of EU-Eco-Audit Regulation (EMAS I).
1996	Commencement of the worldwide applicable environmental management system DIN EN ISO 14001.
2001	Environmental Management Systems become accepted and state of the art; Launch of EMAS II.
2002	World Summit on Sustainable Development (WSSD) in Johannesburg takes stock of international sustainable achievements.

Source: compiled by the author

In the course of time the consideration of business that 'environmentalism costs money' could be turned into opposite. In line with the development of environmental protection new concepts appeared. Production integrated measures and the idea of production optimisation respectively efficiency enforced the success of environmental awareness in business. In line with global environmental problems and increasing social tensions the claim for an applicable approach prevailed. The concept of sustainable development schedules here.

2.2 Sustainable development

The term 'sustainable development' remains until today vague and is connected with different contents. The term is often used as new, modern phrase for an environmental acceptable development and therewith is shortened perspicuously in its content and claim.

Sustainable development is a socio-political approach whereby on the one hand chances of future generations will not deteriorate compared to possibilities of present generations (intergenerational equity) and whereby on the other hand a balance should be reached between poor and rich countries (intragenerational equity).[4] Accordingly sustainable management differs ecological, economic and social sets of problems and fields of activities. These columns are described according to *Balderjahn* as in the following:[5]

a) The ecological dimension is considered in science and in public. This goes back to the rational background and the therewith connected measurability. The ecological dimension covers environmental protection. It reaches out for e.g. the minimisation of the resource input respectively the material flow rate. As well it considers the environmental impact e.g. through emissions and the minimisation of potential dangers e.g. through operating actions. Thereby a systematic minimisation of ecological impact and risks in all departments and throughout the whole product life cycle is requested.

---

[4] Cp. *Balderjahn, Ingo,* Nachhaltiges Marketing-Management, Lucius&Lucius Verlagsgesellschaft mbH, Stuttgart, 2004, p. 1
[5] Cp. Ibid., p. 9 et seqq.

b) The social dimension is up to now of lower significance. It mainly covers questions of intragenerational equity. Basically it deals with the implementation of solidarity. Consequently it is associated with the distribution of prosperity and overall chances for living. It can as well concentrate on single aspects of life quality such as health and education issues on local, national and international levels. In context this dimension measures the social acceptability of corporate action, and includes relationship management to stakeholders.

c) The economic dimension is less well-defined. It is mostly applied for solution finding of intergenerational diversification difficulties. Thereby this dimension covers on the one hand the implementation of societal and ecological claims through corporate actions in order to gain competitive advantage. On the other hand the macroenvironmental context contains possibilities for business to contribute to e.g. the creation of jobs, appropriate prosperity and humane life standards for mankind.

Table 2-2 mirrors further dimensional criteria, which are based on the sustainability check developed by *future e.V.*. *John Elkington* assumes in its "triple-bottom-line" concept that between the three dimensions inter-relations exist, which influence each other in multiple ways. Ecology and economy can only keep in balance if social aims are considered at the same time. Thus economic growth cannot be achieved in long-term if social peace is disturbed and environment is destroyed. Ecological claims have only then an opportunity if the economic as well as the social scope are intact.[6]

To satisfy the needs of the present generation without compromising the ability of future generations to meet their own needs, it is indispensable to integrate all dimensions for long-term success. An isolated consideration is not recommendable; however corporations do not yet consider the three dimensions equally. Each business is affected respectively concerned to a different extent in the ecological, economic or social context. Its industry affiliation influences thereby the progress about the implementation of the particular dimension.

---

[6] Cp. *Hardtke, Arnd; Prehn, Marco* (Ed.), Perspektiven der Nachhaltigkeit, Vom Leitbild zur Erfolgsstrategie, Betriebswirtschaftlicher Verlag Dr. Th. Gabler GmbH, Wiesbaden, 2001, p. 59

Table 2-2: Sustainability Check

• Ecological criteria	Sound exposure to resources, Reduction of environmental burden by furnishes, Minimisation of risks for human and environment, Environmental sound products and processes, Global ecological responsibility.
• Economic criteria	Long-term licence to operate, Added value and fair distribution, Orientation to needs, Local/ global responsibility.
• Social criteria	Assurance of work and training positions/ employee interests, Encouragement of work safety and health, Equality of man and woman, Social considerateness, Global responsibility.

Source: Translated acc. to *Balderjahn*, p. 12 et seq.

2.3 Marketing and sustainability

Most descriptions of marketing focus on satisfaction of needs and on market orientation, thus *Kotler* defines marketing as "a social and managerial process by which individuals and groups obtain what they need and want through creating and exchanging products and values with others."[7] Besides marketing is often connected with unlimited growth, extension of markets, increase of market segments and creation of new marketing opportunities. The *American Marketing-Association* (*AMA*) extended the definition of marketing in 2004 to "an organizational function and a set of processes for creating, communicating and delivering value to customers and for managing customer relationships in ways that benefit the organization and its stakeholders."

Independent of the term sustainability literature discusses societal and ecological challenges for a couple of years and therewith argues if the practiced marketing provides an appropriate concept respectively instruments for these challenges.

---
[7] Cp. *Kotler, Philip et al.*, Principles of Marketing, 2nd European ed., Prentice Hall Inc, New Jersey/ USA, 1999, p. 10

The study 'Marketing and Environment' in 1979 published by Hans Raffée emphasized the responsibility of marketing for various ecological consequences caused by industry and economy. Raffée therein claims businesses to integrate the ecological aspect and to thrive environmental awareness. Nevertheless Raffée recognized the risks of such an 'eco movement' which is as well combined with new doubtful product variations. Thus Raffée asks businesses to analyse their products in terms of environmental compatibility and to publish adequate information for consumers. In the mid 1980ies new applicable marketing concepts appeared. On the one side they focussed on commercial marketing for environmental products, on the other side they referred to a non-commercial marketing for the area of environmental protection. The scientific debate claims for commercial eco-marketing a stronger involvement of ecology into the overall concept of a business as well as an integrated environmental management orientation. For the operational implementation an ecological marketing mix is needed, as Meffert illustrates in figure 2-1. So far ecological oriented marketing could establish.

Figure 2-1: Approaches for an ecological oriented marketing mix

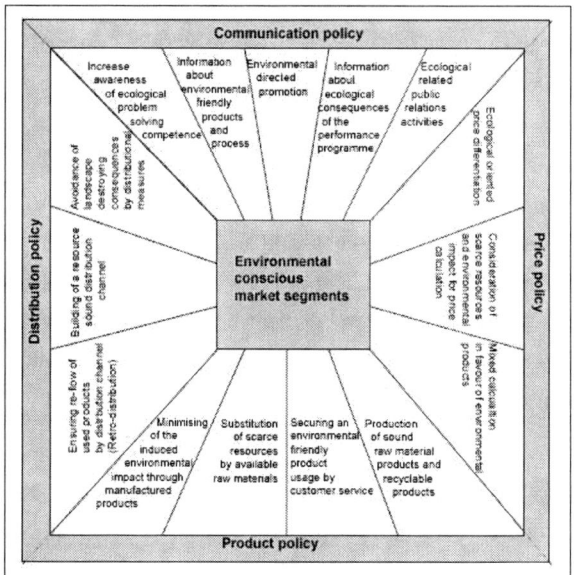

Source: Translated acc. to Meffert/Kirchgeorg, l.c. p. 285

By orienting on ecological and economic aspects it neglects the third dimension of 'social' aspects. Sustainable oriented marketing schedules here, and the question arises how marketing can pick up the concept of sustainability to give consideration to the claims of sustainable development.

According to *Kirchgeorg* sustainable marketing should refer to planning, coordination, implementation and control of all market and societal related exchange processes to prevent or reduce ecological and social problems. It therewith targets on realizing the focussed business objectives by competitive advantage, by assurance of the societal legitimacy and by a permanent satisfaction of needs from the actual and potential customers. Marketings' core task consists in combining environmental, social and competitive advantages by innovative strategies. Here strategies are included which enable a change of market related general frameworks and thus lead to an encouragement of sustainable oriented market performances.[8]

Sustainable oriented marketing needs to consider the inside-out as well as the outside-in perspective. For all actions the society and not the market is reference point. In other words sustainable marketing needs to adapt the socio-political approach of sustainability and needs to orient activities towards the requirements of market, society and natural environment in equal measure.[9] This orientation should be regarded for each entrepreneurial action of the various areas. Figure 2-2 reflects that sustainable aspects must be integrated in all departments. In line *Belz* claims that sustainable marketing needs to strive for a change of political and public frameworks to create or improve the required conditions for a successful introduction of ecological and social acceptable products respectively services in the total market.[10] This integrative approach conforms to the concept of the mega-marketing-mix by *Kotler*, in which the operational instruments are as well extended to 'politics' and 'public opinion'.[11] In context of this study the operational level of

---

[8] Cp. *Kichgeorg, Manfred*, Nachhaltigkeits- Marketing, in: UmweltWirtschaftsForum, 2002, Magazine No. 4, p. 4 - 11.
[9] Cp. *Balderjahn, Ingo*, Nachhaltiges Marketing-Management, Lucius&Lucius Verlagsgesellschaft mbH, Stuttgart, 2004 p. 39 et seqq.
[10] Cp. *Belz, Frank-Martin*, Integratives Öko-Marketing. Erfolgreiche Vermarktung ökologischer Produkte und Leistungen, Deutscher Universitäts-Verlag GmbH, Betriebswirtschaftlicher Verlag Dr. Th. Gabler GmbH, 1. Aufl., Wiesbaden, 2001, l.c. p. 97
[11] Cp. *Wüstenhagen, Rolf, Villiger, Alex, Meyer, Arnt*, Jenseits der Öko-Nische, Birkhäuser Verlag AG, Basel, 2000, p. 50

sustainable marketing relates to the ecological marketing instruments and will only present sustainable actions within this scope.

Figure 2-2: Areas of sustainable oriented marketing

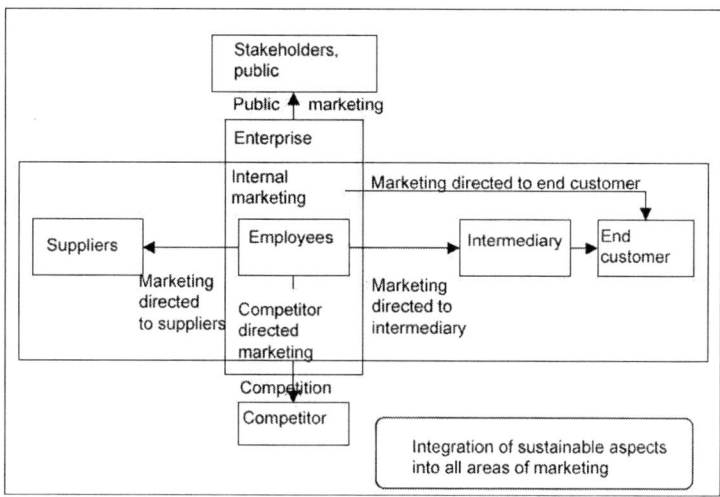

Source: acc. to the integrated marketing approach of *Meffert*, compiled by the author, l.c. p. 27

3 Awareness and behaviour

Production and consumption patterns of industrial states are supposed to be the main indicator for the worldwide progressing environmental pollution. The *German Federal Environmental Agency* estimates that 30 to 40% of the pollution derive directly and indirectly from domestic consumption. Individual consumption presents an enormous potential for the reduction of environmental impact and social problems. Thus consumers hold a key role for innovation and diffusion of sustainable products and services.[12] If the target is thus set on the encouragement of sustainable consumption patterns, the question arises to which extent consumers are actually prepared and able to design their individual consumption in regard to sustainability. Which movements will thereby influence the consumers in future and which different characteristics does the modern consumer type show off? This and similar questions should be analysed in the following.

---

[12] Cp. Ibid., p.136 et seqq.

3.1 Attempt to define sustainable oriented consumption

The term of sustainable consumption is until now not foreseen by any unique definition. The variety of expressions which are associated with sustainable consumption such as 'ecological', 'social acceptable', 'ethical', 'political' or 'responsible' clarify the necessity for a differentiated consideration.

Consumers need to be informed before and during the purchase decision about proper usage and about the adequate disposal of goods. Correspondingly these categories are valid for services. Besides this core area of consumer counselling further areas arise in scope of sustainable orientation. These areas can be described in terms of abdication of consumption, reflection of need, longer usage and 'using instead of possessing'.[13]

In line basic values need to be changed, so that sustainable consumption can be understood as a new kind of quality. Therefore it is as well indispensable to include attributes of the up and downstream processes of raw material sourcing, production and disposal similar to the importance of the usual consumers' purchase criteria (e.g. quality, price and prestige).

Sustainable consumption deals thereby besides ecological dimensions with social and ethical questions, such as humane and healthy working conditions. In line *Schönheit* from the *Institute for Market and Environment* (*Imug*) describes sustainable consumption as "political consume, in which individual consumers can exert influence on the global set of problems by their purchase decisions."[14] Thus consumers' decisive criteria orient on various socio-political interests, which are mostly brought up in line with events by the corresponding initiatives or organisations. For example in times of the first Gulf war the German consumer protection called to boycott those businesses which participated in the armament of Iraq. The humane society publishes annually a list to highlight those businesses who refuse animal testing. The '*E-quality*' certificate for women friendly companies and the '*transfair*' label for goods made under socially acceptable conditions are further

---

[13] Cp. *Lübke, Volkmar*, Informationskonzepte für einen nachhaltigen Konsum, in: *Linne, Gudrun, Schwarz, Michael (ed.)*, Handbuch Nachhaltige Entwicklung: Wie ist nachhaltiges Wirtschaften machbar?, Verlag Leske + Budrich, Opladen, 2003, p. 112

[14] Cp. *Müller, Edda*, „Nachhaltiger Konsum: Utopie oder Geschäftsstrategie?", Rede auf dem Forum Nachhaltigkeit, Veranstalter: American Chamber of Commerce in Germany (AmCham Germany) am 12. April 2005 in Berlin

examples of initiatives that discovered the socio-political relevance of the purchase decision.[15]

In spite of its fuzziness the term 'sustainable consumption' should be carried on in the following in line with *Balderjahn* who defines sustainable consumption as consume which "satisfies own needs and demands without reducing life and consumption possibilities of other humans as well as those of future generations. Sustainable consumption refers besides the satisfaction of the individual needs and demands to the environmental protection as well as to the needs and demands of other people."[16]

3.2 General mood of consumers

The social scientist *B. Michael* classifies the development of environmental awareness into five categories for Germany. At the beginning of the 1970ies publics' environmental interest arose from scientific studies and discussions which regarded the quality of life. Phase 2 at the end of the 1970ies is characterised by the formation of awareness towards environmental changes, so that legislation passed first bills. In the beginning of the 1980ies environmental awareness changed to proactive environmental protection (phase 3) which was influenced by non-governmental organisations such as *Greenpeace*. Their actions were supported by public due to increasing environmental problems and scandals. The peak of international environmental protection was reached at the end of the 1980ies. Here dramatic changes in consumer behaviour can be detected and an increase of environmental friendly products in markets followed (phase 4). For the 1990ies *B. Michael* predicted a phase characterised by environmental hysteria.[17]

15 year later: the expected dramatic legislation became partly true but environmental harmful products did not disappear on markets. Indeed environmental awareness decreased during the 1990ies, but primary the *German Federal Environmental*

---

[15] Cp. *Lübke, Volkmar,* Informationskonzepte für einen nachhaltigen Konsum, in: *Linne, Gudrun, Schwarz, Michael (ed.),* Handbuch Nachhaltige Entwicklung: Wie ist nachhaltiges Wirtschaften machbar?, Verlag Leske + Budrich, Opladen, 2003, l.c., p. 110
[16] Cp. *Balderjahn, Ingo,* Nachhaltiges Marketing-Management, Lucius&Lucius Verlagsgesellschaft mbH, Stuttgart, 2004, p.136
[17] Cp. *Meffert, Heribert, Kirchgeorg, Manfred,* Marktorientiertes Umweltmanagement, Schäffer Poeschel Verlag, Stuttgart, 3. rev. Ed., 1998, p. 13

Agency could determine an increase of the topics' importance in the surveys of 2004 and 2006. The individual orientations and values which are uttered in questions of environmental protection and sustainability prove an environmental proactive attitude. Table 3-1 shows five different general moods of citizens.

Table 3-1: Environmental attitudes of consumers

Type 1 (37%)	"I organise my life preferably environmental friendly, even if it is hard but I want to be a role model." Motto: Start with yourself, do not wait for others.
Type 2 (42%)	"You should not exaggerate, but environmental protection relates to fairness and civic duty." Motto: No extremes – everyone needs to take part in.
Type 3 (16%)	"Individuals provoke only little when saving energy or cutting down car driving." Motto: What makes the difference if nothing is done on the top?
Type 4 (4%)	"You'll never know, environmental catastrophes, etc." Motto: In spite of all enjoy life, there is no sense in pessimism.
Type 5 (1%)	"It's not that bad, the topic of environmental pollution is going overboard." Technique will get it fixed." Motto: If we are alright, then environment is okay as well.

Source: Translated acc. to *Bundesministerium für Umwelt, Naturschutz und Reaktorsicherheit* (Ed.), Umweltbewusstsein 2002, p. 29

Thereby 37% of the respondents join the group of the "pro-environmental" attitude. Whereas Type 2 and Type 3 may be summarized to the group of "ambivalent characters", to which 58% of respondents belong. At least 5% of the respondents renounce any environmental problems.

All questioned citizens faced statements from the area of disposal, energy, mobility, consumption and commitment. A careful exposure to waste is for the majority of the respondents the most important subject area. Thereby waste separation and the saving of needless packaging material are the basics of the quoted actions. The saving of energy resources is of equal significance. The mobility sector reveals the known dispute between the usage of cars and the public transport: the intention to make short trips by no-frills airlines rises from 15% in 2002 to 28% in 2006.

However 45% of the respondents want to commit to environmental protection and 63% are of the opinion that their social environment would appreciate such an engagement. People are indeed aware of environmental protection. But only a minority group is prepared to integrate sustainable elements into their own behaviour.

Social networks herein influence the attitude towards environmental commitment; and thus sustainability could proceed to the public debate.[18]

In times of internalisation German consumers are of importance as well as the citizenship abroad and their environmental behaviour. The *Gesellschaft für Konsumforschung* (*Gfk*) in Nuremberg detected environmental active consumers in Germany and Denmark, and only a few in Belgium and in the Netherlands. Consequently criterions for sustainable purchase behaviour depend on culture and country.[19] International marketing concepts are hardly applicable and sustainable orientated marketing needs to be set up for the specific region. More consumers can be met by a comprehensive and confidential information policy. Appropriate intermediaries and multipliers are needed so that various consumers types (cp. Chapter 3.4) are obtained. Hereunto the Anglo-Saxon movement of *'Lifestyle of Health and Sustainability'* (*LOHAS*) which demands healthy and ecological products respectively services approaches a starting point.[20]

3.3 Purchase criteria

The survey of *Environmental Awareness 2006* reveals citizens' willingness to integrate sustainable consumption. 68% of the respondents are aware of their influencing role and believe they can contribute to environmental protection by their purchase behaviour.[21]

By questioning criteria for sustainable purchase decisions most consumers are geared on durability respectively long life ability (90%) as well as on energy consumption (84%). A low relevance for decision making comes up to the 'boycott of environmental harming businesses' (45%) as well as 'the purchase of labelled goods' (41%). The respondents attribute even lower significance to the manufacturers' engagement in environmental and social aspects (34%).[22] These favoured product

---

[18] Cp. *Bundesministerium für Umwelt, Naturschutz und Reaktorsicherheit* (Ed.), Umweltbewusstsein 2006, Berlin, 2006, p. 64
[19] Cp. *Balderjahn, Ingo,* Nachhaltiges Marketing-Management, Lucius&Lucius Verlagsgesellschaft mbH, Stuttgart, 2004, p. 150
[20] Cp. *Troge, Andreas,* Nachhaltiger Konsum – Illusion der Ökos?, Speech on the symposium of 'GRÜN leben', Berlin, 9.12.2006
[21] Cp. *Bundesministerium für Umwelt, Naturschutz und Reaktorsicherheit* (Ed.), Umweltbewusstsein 2006, Berlin, 2006, l.c. p. 17
[22] Cp. Ibid., p. 65

attributes indicate as well the associations to 'sustainable purchase behaviour'. Moreover the study reveals that 69% are prepared to pay more for fair traded products (thereof 20% are 'very' prepared) and 66% are prepared to accept higher prices for less environmental harming products (thereof 12% are 'very' prepared).[23] However the acceptance of higher prices depends on the kind of product. Health and environmental acceptable attributes are important for products of daily usage. According to figure 3-2 the consideration of health and environmental aspects could persuade in the field of detergents. Whereas a small number goes for conventional food and cosmetics. In the field of energy 57% of respondents agree that consumers' are challenged to save energy resources, but indeed 88% do not consider the purchase of green power.[24]

Consequently consumers are ambivalent. There are gaps between the attitude and the actual consumption behaviour, one often speaks about the 'free rider-problem'.

Table 3-2: Purchase criteria

Amount in %	Survey 2006				
	A very big role	A rather big role	A rather small role	No role	Average value
For purchasing cleaning agents health and environmental aspects play...	21	44	26	8	2,21
The usage of organic varnish in my living rooms plays for me....	15	35	31	19	2,58
For my nourishment organic food plays a...	10	28	47	15	2,67
If cosmetics are made mainly out of natural ingredients does play...	12	29	34	25	2,72

Source: translated acc. to. *Bundesministerium für Umwelt, Naturschutz und Reaktorsicherheit* (2006)

To advance sustainable consumption mainly policy is asked for consistent and concretised measures as well as for recommendations. An approach can be seen in the development of the 'sustainable basket of goods' developed by *Imug* and the *Council on Sustainable Development*. Here sustainable alternatives are suggested for all 750 products listed in the conventional basket of the *Federal Statistical Office*.

---

[23] Cp. Ibid., p. 66 et seq.
[24] Cp. Ibid., p. 29 et seqq.

Thereby the published results reveal that sufficient products and services exist on markets which can be combined with the objectives of sustainable consumption.[25]

3.4 Typology of consumers

Environmental awareness was a topic of the well educated class from the 1980ies to the mid 1990ies. In the beginning of the 21st century it is a topic independent of social status. The alternative 'tree huggers' managed to establish the topic in areas of policy, economy, science, law, churches and media. Ecology became a social norm and is topic in all social classes.[26]

Social science herein contributes to the consumption research by regarding customers' orientation, values and attitudes while purchasing. So called 'life style' analyses express the social and psychological identity of a consumer as well as they symbolize the consumers' belonging to one group respectively the social distance to others. The *Institute for Social- and Ecological Science* (*ISOE*) analysed German consumption types and styles in terms of sustainability. One prevailing typology can be found in the publication of *Claudia Empacher*. Her clustering is based on a multidimensional consumption style built by the social situation of the household, the consumption orientations and the actual consumption behaviour.[27] Consequently ten basic consumption models are build up. Figure 3-1 gives a short overview about these ten consumer types and their consumption attitudes.

Figure 3-1: Customer typology

Group 1 "The environmental accessible"

Type 1 "Fully-managed eco-families"
- One or more children, both parents employed, financial better off.
- Shortage of time provokes liability to convenience products, thus sustainable orientation as time permits
- Openness towards unknown, orientation towards ethical aspects, integral orientation towards health

Type 2 "Every day-life artists"
- Younger people, mostly women in social or artistically vocations, moderate income
- Creative, tend to handicrafts and often customize second-hand bought products
- Strong interest in environmental topics
- Orientation towards ethical aspects and health

---

[25] Cp. *Burger, Katrin*, Politik mit der Einkaufstüte, in: die Tageszeitung, Berlin, Bonn, 02.04.2003
[26] Cp. *Stäsche, Peter*, Bio - gestern und heute, in: *Markt & Medien*, 2007, Magazine No. 3, p. 1
[27] Cp. *Empacher, Claudia*, Zielgruppenspezifische Potentiale und Barrieren für nachhaltigen Konsum – Ergebnisse einer sozial-ökologischen Konsumentenuntersuchung, in: *Weber, Christoph, Scherhorn, Gerhard* (Ed.), Nachhaltiger Konsum – Auf dem Weg zur gesellschaftlichen Verankerung, oekom Verag, München, 2003, p.455 et seq.

Group 2 "The privileged"

Type 3 "Childless professionals"
- Successful professionals singles or childless couples, high income
- Strong orientation towards convenience products
- Exclusive consumer products (e.g. big cars or multiple long-range trips p.a.)
- Quality and Service is of special importance, women are orientated towards health

Type 4 "Status-orientated privileged families"
- Very wealthy families, husband holds down an occupation while wife accepts representative and charitable functions
- High consumption level, status and classiness are of special importance
- Relationships in the same privileged milieu, hence hardly accessible for ecological orientated strategies
- General disinterest of societal, political or environmental topics

Group 3 "The hardly accessible overstrained"

Type 5 "Underprivileged who can't cope"
- Unemployed, single parents or elderly people, less income
- Commodity products to cover societal status (tend to purchase cheap and short-life products)
- Little time and little social contacts make these consumers inaccessible for environmental topics

Type 6 "People fed up with consumption"
- Mostly male divorcees, singles or women who refuse housework
- Reduction of housework to minimum (due to negative attitude) and
- strong orientation towards convenience products as well as making use of external services
- Environmental protection is considered as impertinence

Type 7 "Self-interested youngsters"
- Adolescent persons as well as young grown-ups, low budget
- First own household, overstrained and strong orientation towards convenience products
- Adventure orientated and influenced by circle of friends

Group 4 "The ambivalent traditionalists"

Type 8 "Rural traditionalists"
- Elderly married couples, families with children in homestead, rural or provincial environment, traditional role allocation
- Involvement in community, bound in regional and in social direct environment, as well as orientated towards regional products

Type 9 "Run-off-the-mill families"
- Families with traditional role allocation, in the East of Germany women are employed
- Inconspicuous consumption patterns, orientated towards mainstream
- Economized, non lavishing and orientated in quality

Type 10 "Active seniors"
- Elderly retired people, fit and a good financial budget
- Cosmopolitanism and demand to discover new ventures
- Same consumption patterns like "rural traditionalists"
- Sufficient time resources makes them a potential contact for ecological orientated strategies

Source: Translated acc. to. *Empacher*, p. 455-467

Here it needs to be added that one faces a new type of consumer. *Wüstenhagen et al.* speak of the segment of 'situation specific accessible consumers' which does not reject ecology but values the satisfaction of other needs to the same extent. This hybrid consumer with its diametrically opposed attitudes and behaviour patterns challenges marketing. High market shares can be reached if marketing succeeds in combining different product attributes and if more than one consumer demand is communicated.[28]

Marketing needs to focus on the improvement of the sustainable products' image and on the development of corresponding services in order to enforce sustainable consumption patterns. Therefore the typology reveals some indicators for target group specific potentials as well as it reveals barriers of sustainable consumption patterns. It needs to be noted that such segmentations based on general moods, purchase criteria and customer typologies help to choose the particular marketing instruments.

3.5 Retail and competition behaviour

Retail is of further significance for successful introduction of sustainable products. Because it is able to bottle the market entry of environmental sound products or support social acceptable products. In context of retails' power one often speaks about its gate-keeper function. This calls for educating retail about its importance in aspects of sustainable products. At the same time it preconditions education about its specific environmental problems which e.g. occur while warehousing, transporting or selling the product. Besides it is of necessity that environmental legislation which affects retail is known. Moreover businesses should focus on co-operative aspects with when designing environmental and social acceptable product variants. First of all data for retails' ecological competence should be allocated for a possible segmentation of potential retailers especially in regard to a qualified advisory service.[29]

Next to watching retails' behaviour it is indispensable to analyse competitors' ecological oriented performance. By well directed measures of one competitor, the

---

[28] Cp. *Wüstenhagen, Rolf, Villiger, Alex, Meyer, Arnt,* Jenseits der Öko-Nische, Birkhäuser Verlag AG, Basel, 2000, p. 296 et seqq.
[29] Cp. *Meffert, Heribert, Kirchgeorg, Manfred,* Marktorientiertes Umweltmanagement, Schäffer Poeschel Verlag, Stuttgart, 3. rev. Ed., 1998, l.c., p. 98.

marketing conditions can change dramatically in a short period of time. For each industry it is thus necessary to obtain the following market data (see figure 3-2):

- Danger of market entry from new competitors,
- Threat of backup products,
- Degree of competitors' affectedness in sourcing, distributing and disposal of products, e.g. through environmental legislation and an increasing demand of environmental oriented solutions,
- Competitors preparedness for co-operating in order to work out a joint solution of the industries' ecological challenges,
- Extent of rivalry among businesses of one industry through enforcement of environmental sound products and offensive communication policy.[30]

Figure 3-3 comprises the dominating driving power of the textile and clothing industry. The direction of the arrows corresponds to the applied pressure, while the thickness of the arrows indicates the significance of competition throughout the industry. Ecological aspects are of low importance; mainly public pressure in terms of social aspects can be detected while consumers focus on the health acceptability of products to an increased extent. Here appropriate developed product features (which combine ecological and health aspects) enable market newcomers to open up an established market. A well-known example from another industry is the successful market launch of the detergent agent '*Frosch*', which shifted its product attributes to better environmental acceptability in the phase of increasing environmental awareness at the late 1980ies. In the same way suppliers increase their bargaining power towards customers when increasing the range of environmental sound raw materials or preliminary products. The customer can on the other side put pressure on the manufacturer when offering solely environmental harmful product variations (e.g. CFC in fridges or aerosol cans).[31]

---

[30] Cp. Ibid., l.c., p. 99
[31] Cp. Ibid., l.c., p.100

Figure 3-2: Dimensions of an ecological oriented competitive analysis

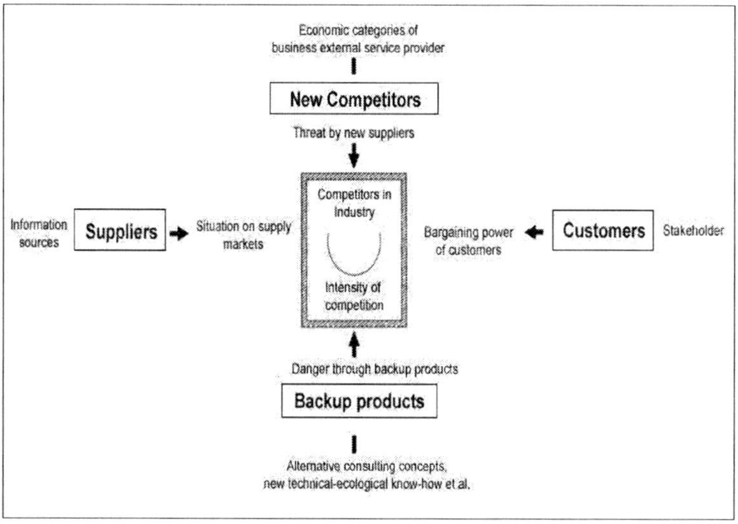

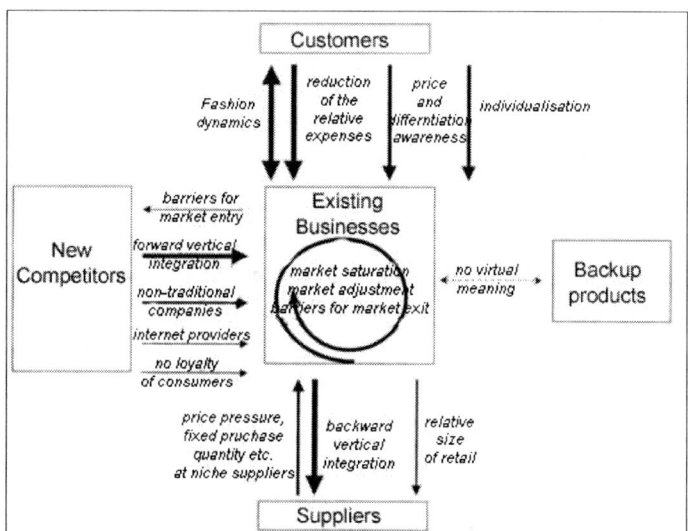

Source: Translated acc. to Meffert/Kirchgeorg, l.c., p. 103

Figure 3-3: Competitive movers in apparel retail industry

Source: Translated acc. to *Wüstenhagen et al.*, l.c., p. 158

4 Markets

In the last few years international markets approached spaciously as well as culturally. The internet connects people from regions all over the world; cellular phones make sure that you are accessible anywhere and anytime. Globalisation and deregulation provoked a dramatic extension of selling and buying markets. Merging of enterprises from home and foreign countries resulted in the formation of technology partners, joint ventures or tie-ups. Furthermore enterprises execute acquisitions abroad to enforce their own market penetration.[32] Here the pharmaceutical and chemical industry attracted attention in the last decade. Both Suisse enterprises *Ciba Geigy* and *Sandoz* merged to the global chemical and biotechnological market leader which is named *Novartis*. The American enterprise *Pfizer* is on the top of the worldwide ranking by acquiring its competitors *Warner-Lambert* and *Pharmacia*. Both examples show how some enterprises proceed in enlarging their global business networks. In contrast the chemical business *BASF* sold its pharmaceutical section to the American enterprise *Abbott*. The concentration on the core business enabled *BASF* to succeed in penetrating the chemical industry and in consolidating its market position.[33]

But what is happening on the market for ecological products?

Markets for environmental friendly products can be divided in two categories. On the one hand there is a market for environmental technologies, on the other hand there is a market for environmental sound products. This classification is essential because demand and supply differ dramatically. The market for environmental technology is rather heterogeneous and orientated towards the individual customer. The increase of environmental legislations results in an increased level of environmental technologies. The market is dominated by small to medium businesses. To comply with the dynamic market of environmental technologies it is necessary that such companies provide the willingness for innovations, flexibility and know how.[34] One

---

[32] Cp. *Zimmermann, Rolf*, New Business Style, Gellius Verlag GmbH, Herrsching am Ammersee, 2005, p. 16 et seqq.
[33] Cp. *Hoffritz, Jutta:* Eine Pille gegen Einsamkeit, in: DIE ZEIT, 28.09.2006, Nr. 40
[34] Cp. *Türck, Rainer*, Das ökologische Produkt, Verlag Wissenschaft & Praxis, Ludwigsburg/Berlin, 2. Auflage, 1991, p. 170

example can be found in the research of favourable material for the production of solar panels.

However this study deals with the market for environmental and social acceptable products. Predominantly small companies offered ecological oriented products, e.g. health-food and whole food shops sold high quality products in a high price segment to a limited customer group. Ecology was a topic for niche markets.[35] By the rising environmental awareness and the willingness of consumers to purchase environmental acceptable products a market potential for big as well as for small business developed. Some small pioneer business could enlarge their market position and penetrate the commodity market, whereas others were partly surprised by the assertiveness of eco products and could not maintain their market position.

4.1 Market participants

The specific marketing situation differs for various enterprises and its products. The situation depends on internal and external facts. External facts are e.g. customer structure and behaviour, growth rate of the industry, nature of demand, competition relations or legal framework. Internal variables are on the other hand e.g. funds (respectively the marketing budget), sales organisation, manufacturing capacity or the type and function of the offered performances. *Meffert* allocates factors which determine the situation into certain criteria and thereby a situation analysis by means of the criteria market, market participant, marketing instruments (marketing mix) and environment (here it needs to be understand in a broader sense). *Meffert* allocates to the criteria environment these reference points: nature, economy, society, technology as well as law and policy.[36]

Marketing management performs the task of determining the direction and strength of factors in certain decision situations and eventually resolve necessary changes.[37]

---

[35] Cp. *Wüstenhagen, Rolf, Villiger, Alex, Meyer, Arnt,* Jenseits der Öko-Nische, Birkhäuser Verlag AG, Basel, 2000, l.c. p. 20
[36] Cp. *Meffert, Heribert,* Marketing: Grundlagen der Absatzpolitik, Gabler-Verlag, Wiesbaden, 7. rev. Ed, 1993, l.c., p. 57 et seq.
[37] Cp. *Meffert, Heribert,* Marketing: Grundlagen der Absatzpolitik, Gabler-Verlag, Wiesbaden, 7. rev. Ed, 1993, l.c., p. 57 et seq.

Table 4-1: Example of a situational analysis in marketing

Components of a situation analysis	Benchmark	Important determination Factors
Market	Total Market (Product classes)	Development Growth Elasticity
	Industrial Market (Product group)	Development status Saturation degree Market allocation
	(Product-related)	Structure of needs Degree of substitution Product concentration
Market participants	Manufacturer	Market position Product and range orientation Supply concentration
	Competitor	Competitor strength Differentiation degree Range concentration
	Intermediary	Functional performance Product range structure Market coverage
	Facilitators	Functional performance
	Consumer	Demand situation Buying power Attitude

Source: translated and modified acc. to. *Meffert*, l.c., p. 58

A survey of environmental protection in the area of Baden-Wuerttemberg questioned circa 300 businesses 'which market participants could contribute to environmental protection?'. These businesses considered consumers (ca. 16%) as the one who could contribute most. The same contribution could derive from manufacturers (14%) by volunteer measures and retail (14%) by corresponding environmental aware product range. Less contribution could come from consumer associations, mass media and state (all between 12-13%) by informational measures and legislation. Trade associations (9%) and policy (8%) were named as the ones who could contribute to lowest extent.[38] However it needs to be noted that all market participants are expected to contribute to sustainable development and that all are challenged to evaluate and to improve their contribution to society and to environment.

---

[38] Cp. *Grettenberger, Dunja*, Umweltschutz und Umweltbewusstsein, Ansatzpunkte einer effizienten Umweltpolitik, Verlag Wissenschaft und Praxis, Berlin, 1996, l.c. p. 184 et seq.

4.2 Challenges

Retail adopts as so called gatekeeper a significant position to link manufacturers and consumers. Retail decides if and which products are added to the product range. The mergence to some trade chains resulted in an even increasing significance of retail. In scope of the strong buyers' power some manufacturers do hard in realizing their sustainable oriented marketing concepts. According to Meffert and Kirchgeorg three possible implementation alternatives exist:

- Ecological orientated retail directed approach
- Ecological orientated consumption directed approach
- Vertical integrated approach.

The retail-directed approach or ecology push strategy concentrates solely on retail, which endangers manufacturers to face a partner with lacking cooperativeness. This approach misses a communicational concept for consumers, which results in listing problems and a non-existing acceptance of eco products by retail.

Whereas the end consumer is reached by manufacturers in the consumption directed approach (respectively marketing pull) but with weak support from retail. As mentioned above awareness and purchasing patterns of consumers differ so that retail does not adapt all goods to its product range. Manufacturers will only succeed in implementing their marketing concept through a co-operation with retail in line with the vertical integrated approach. Both market participants should unfold their strategies when co-operating[39] which is further illuminated in chapter 6.

Retail began to install a withdrawal system for packaging in the last decade. Successful innovations comprise e.g. the reuse of bottles, the controlled disposal of batteries, used oil or electronic devices such as computers. Besides consumers demand additional service regarding the environmental quality, the usage and the manufacturing process of a product. Thereby salespersons adopt an important position to thwart discrepancies between the attitude and the purchase behaviour. Profound knowledge is required from employees. In scope retail needs to invest in employees' education and needs to update sales persons permanently about

---
[39] Cp. *Meffet, Heribert, Kirchgeorg, Manfred*, Marktorientiertes Umweltmanagement, Schäffer Poeschel Verlag, Stuttgart, 3. rev. Ed., 1998 p. 240

environmental compatibility and environmental usage of the product. One approach for employee training is developed by the *German Federal Foundation for Environment*. In line with this concept an industry specific homepage provides information about sustainable product ranges and customer service. The combination of a training software with an adaptable instruction of employee training and an online information pool should support small enterprises on their way to an ecological acceptable and sustainable development.[40]

As mentioned above the sales conversation should mainly put ecological and social topics in foreground while the design of the shop inheres to transmit the ecological relevant product- and usage information. This may be communicated by display and merchandising materials to close the existing information gap of environmental sound packaging ideas. Sponsoring especially with reference to local environmental or social problems offers an approach for retail to strengthen its trustworthiness. Classic advertisement is going to proceed in future. Hereby it needs to be focussed on securing credibility of the ecological orientated profile and on an authentic communication of the topic.[41]

It is necessary to look at the possibilities of the internet in detail: the significance of retails' distribution networks might be reduced in future and the role of conventional retail might decrease. In scope of this development corresponding measures are indispensable to gain competitive advantage in retail. New chances arise thereby for information transmittance and new individual marketing possibilities can be created to build up a personalised customer relationship. Thus the Suisse grocery enterprise *Coop* uses the internet in an additive role and provides consumers the possibility to research producers of the organic meat.[42]

The worldwide web enables as well manufacturers and consumers to communicate directly. In Austria the online community *Lisa* was initiated to connect the rural agriculture suppliers with the urban high income internet users. Among agriculture associations and initiatives there are small suppliers such as *ATB&G Frenkenberger GmbH* (home delivery of organic food), *'Tischlein Deck Dich'* (organic party service)

---

[40] Cp. *Zentralstelle für Berufsbildung im Einzelhandel e.V.* (Ed.), Available online http://www.elearning.zbb.de (21.01.2007)
[41] Cp. *Meffert, Heribert; Kirchgeorg, Manfred*, Marktorientiertes Umweltmanagement, Schäffer Poeschel Verlag, Stuttgart, 3. rev. Ed., 1998, p. 368
[42] Cp. *Coop* (Ed.), Regionale Produkte, available online http://www.coop.ch/naturaplan/bio_spezialitaeten/regionale_produzenten-de.htm (21.12.2006)

or *'Waldviertel Roggenhof'* (natural after shave and perfumes).[43] In contrast *future e.V.* initiated the project *'texweb'* which uses the internet for the business to business area. Based on the information allocation of four cooperating partners a data base was developed to inform about availability, quality and environmental related attributes of the product. Thereby the project aims on establishing a forum, which specifies the origin of products.[44]

4.3 Industries

The degree to which a business is affected by the public debate on sustainability depends mostly on its industry affiliation. Enterprises which are situated in the primary (e.g. chemistry, paper, energy) and in the pharmaceutical industry are concerned to a higher extent by the debate of sustainable development. Likewise industries are affected which cause high impact through the product usage (e.g. automobile, electronics) or industries which show significant environmental and social risks and/or are cross-linked to other industries (e.g. food, transportation). In contrast enterprises which are situated in the service industry are concerned to a lower extent by the debate of sustainable development. These enterprises provoke low environmental and social impact and/or are rarely chain-linked to other branches (e.g. media, insurances). Furthermore enterprises are rarely concerned when producing a direct environmental and social value (e.g. renewable energy, health services).[45]

The rating of *Bank Sarasin & Cie AG* reflects this and is visualised in figure 4-1. Thereby the rating is a judgement of a industries' total environmental and social risks. It considers categories such as resource consumption and emissions as well as internal and external social conflicts. The overall risk exposition of one industry refers to the results of the analysis of the industries' specific product and its impact throughout the life cycle.[46]

---

[43] available online http://www.lisa.at (21.01.2007)
[44] Cp. *Wüstenhagen, Rolf, Villiger, Alex, Meyer, Arnt,* Jenseits der Öko-Nische, Birkhäuser Verlag AG, Basel, 2000, p. 349
[45] *Bank Sarasin & Cie AG* (Ed.), Mitteilung an die Medien: Im Überblick: die Nachhaltigkeit verschiedener Branchen, Basel, 18.9.2006, n/a.
[46] *Bank Sarasin & Cie AG* (Ed.), Nachhaltigkeitsstudie „Just do it" - aber verantwortungsbewusst, Basel, 2006, l.c., p. 22

Figure 4-1: Sustainable affectedness of various industry

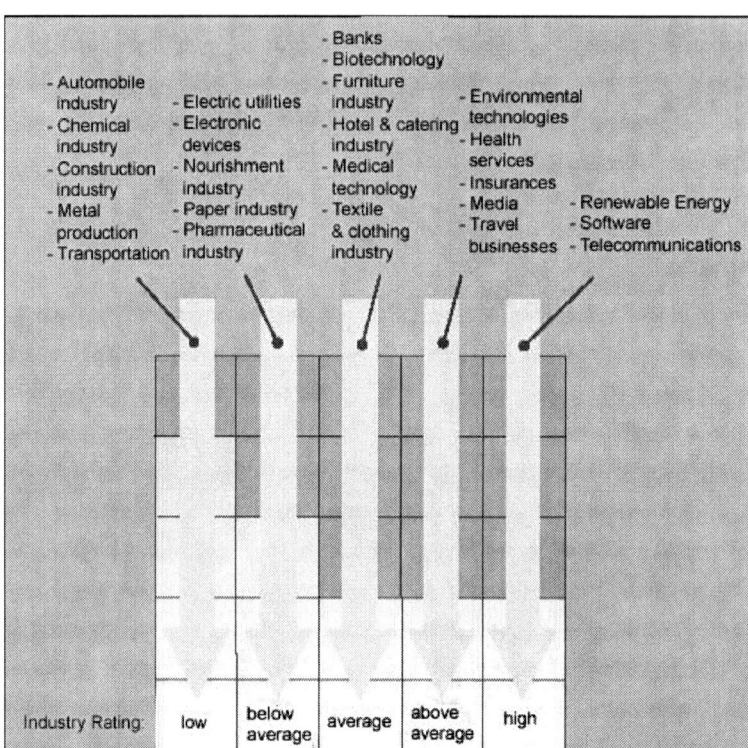

Source: Translated acc. to *Bank Sarasin & Cie AG*, l.c., p. 2

One of the well-known industry, which offers organic goods is the food industry. Although supermarkets are the most popular point of purchase, business giants discover organic products hesitantly. The discount store *Aldi* sold 46% more whole food products than in the previous year 2005. Other retailers such as *Rewe*, *Edeka* or *Kaufland* achieved 64% more turnover through whole food products. In comparison consumer markets such as health food stores or certain whole food shops could increase their turnover by 23%.[47] While the turnover of conventional food products stagnates, organic products become more popular in supermarkets. This market is thus a perfect role model for the textile and clothing industry.

---

[47] Cp. *Wesselmann, Matthias*, Einkauf von Bio-Lebensmitteln: Supermärkte haben die Nase vorn, Press Release, fischerAppelt Kommunikation GmbH, Hamburg, 2006.

Until today ecological mail-order (e.g. *hess natur*) or small pioneer enterprises supplied the market and tried to reach customers by another kind of quality – timeless design with high-quality processing. Pioneer companies thereby are characterised by its idealistic motives and the integration of economic targets (e.g. *Patagonia*). In spite of the pioneers' stronger orientation towards commercial aspects they might be threatened by other participants in the premium segment such as trading concerns. *Coop* launched its *Natura Line* and could therewith double its market share of eco textiles as well as take up the position of the market leader. An increasing orientation towards eco textiles can be detected recently, and the implementation of organic fibres by so called goliath enterprises (e.g. *Wal-Mart, Marks & Spencer*) will enlarge the market share of ecological textiles.[48]

The commodity fashion brands *Marc O'Polo* integrates organic cotton within the product line *'Nature´s Simplicity'* and is prepared to implement the material permanently. By questioning the importance of the ecological attribute *Frauke Geldmancher* Division Head Women of *Marc O'Polo* states that "primarily clothes need to sell about the fitting and the price. The look and the design should suit, by no means clothes may look like 'eco'."[49] In fact clothes need to please, need to communicate vitality and need to be trendy. Thus it appears that a process of rethinking began in the industry, as a 'nice to have' attribute 'green fashion' could penetrate the commercial market.

It is not sufficient to use organic cotton. "As part of development work fair trade should guarantee fair prices for farmers to fight poverty and at the same time offer high-quality products, which are manufactured under ecological and social acceptable criteria"[50] says *Frithjof Schmidt*, member of the European Parliament and correspondent for fair trade. Indeed the buzzword 'ethical fashion brands' comprises labels such as *Edun, Kuyichi* or *Loomstate* which try to acquire customers by design – and at the same sensitise them for the environmental and social set of problems.[51]

---

[48] Cp. *Wüstenhagen, Rolf, Villiger, Alex, Meyer, Arnt*, Jenseits der Öko-Nische, Birkhäuser Verlag AG, Basel, 2000, l.c., p.184
[49] Cp. *Geldmancher, Frauke*, Grünes Bewusstsein – Chance oder Marketinggag? in: X-Ray/global style and fashion, no. 4, B2Bfachverlag gmbH, Salzburg, 2006, p. 24
[50] Cp. *Schmidt, Frithjof*, Fair Trade muss Standard werden, in: X-Ray/ global style and fashion, no. 4, B2Bfachverlag gmbH, Salzburg, 2006, l.c., p. 28
[51] Cp. *Maschewski, Alexandra*, Moralische Mode: Schluss mit Ausreden, rein in die Ökoklamotten, in: DIE WELT, 17.02.2007

In further market segments environmental and social acceptable products penetrate slowly. Thus the brand awareness of *'Moltex eco'* -diapers of the company *Ontex* is significantly lower than the awareness of its competitive conventional products of *Procter & Gamble (Pampers), Fixies GmbH (Fixies)* or *Kimberly & Clark (Huggies)*.

In the market of washing powder some suppliers of 'ecoproducts' can be found. The detergent *Skip* (by *Unilever*) is based on the principle of a modular system. It comprises a basic washing agent, a water softener and a specific sulphide component. This very environmental sound system could not penetrate in the commodity market due to reasons of comfort.

Meanwhile eco detergents are offered by the Belgian company *Ecover* while the manufacturer *Sodosan* is competing on the German market. The commodity market is dominated by three big enterprises *Henkel (Persil, Spee, Weißer Riese), Procter& Gamble (Ariel, Dash, Vizir)* and *Lever Fabergé (Omo, Sunil)*. The recent introduction of detergents in form of tabloids will ignite the debate around the products' environmental compatibility. Whereas environmental sound liquid and super concentrated laundry detergents were introduced by the market leaders such as *Megaperls* of *Henkel* in the last decade, discounters progress in the market of washing tabloids such as *Lidl* by its store brand *'Maxitrat'* or *DM* by *'Denk mit'*. It should be regretted that in 2006 the *German Federal Environmental Agency* recognized an increase of the well tried 'jumbo packets' (higher dosing necessary) in drugstores and supermarkets.[52]

The furniture industry faces no legislative pressure to regard the materials' recycability, its environmental sound processing or the products' positive life cycle analysis. In line with the price pressure many manufacturers shifted production abroad, without being aware that Eastern European and Asian furniture tend to exceed the German mandatory limit values of e.g. formaldehyde or volatile organic compounds. Environmental acceptable products are made by small enterprises such as *Oe.con* or by regional joineries. All over the market share of eco furniture averages in 8%.

Still new materials offer unknown possibilities for the design of ecological furnishing. For example thermoplastic granulates from renewable resources, the so called 'liquid

---

[52] Cp. *Umweltbundesamt* (Ed.), Informationen für Wasch- und Reinigungsmittel 2006, available online http://www.umweltbundesamt.de/uba-info-daten/daten/wasch/trends.htm (21.01.2007)

wood', can imitate plastic shapes without ecological deductions.[53] The Suisse textile finishing company *Rohner Textil AG* offers a furniture covering made from ramie and wool. The automobile business *DaimlerChrysler* applies instead of synthetic fibres implements coconut, flax and latex for the car interior in the South American market. However it needs to be noted that the industry can only proceed in implementing innovative materials if it results in lower prices by remaining or improved quality.

In the market of finance and investments sustainable products can be found to an increased extent. On the one hand there are small banks with limited business circles but good sustainable performance, such as the *EthikBank* or the *UmweltBank AG*. The *EthikBank* guarantees e.g. not to invest in enterprises which are involved in military, nuclear power or genetic engineering. Whereas the *UmweltBank AG* offers ecological oriented insurances. On the other hand internationally-active banks could overcome social and ecological difficulties of their economic activity. Thus the German *Postbank* offers a sustainable fond with the name *Postbank Dynamik Vision*. Investors who attach importance on environmental protection and social responsibility can choose between 30 shares of sustainable enterprises (e.g. *Shimano*) in the *Naturaktienindex NAI*.[54] Fonds in the area of bioenergy represent another market participant in the area of sustainable investment. Thereby investment trusts such as *MTV Capital Invest AG* promote their fond (here the *MTV III Bioenergie Fond*) in order to perceive private funds for the build up of biogas plants.[55]

The energy industry comes up as well with eco power from sun, wind or water. The oligopolistic market is dominated by the enterprises *E.ON*, *RWE*, *EnBW* and *Vattenfall*. These four electricity suppliers offer green power deriving from long existing plants besides niche suppliers such as *Naturstrom AG* or *Greenpeace Energy*.

Ecological computers such as the new product line offered by the multinational enterpise *Fujitsu Siemens* carve out their position on a sustainable oriented consumer market as well as printers and mobile phones. In the same way the

---

[53] Cp. *Mederer, Margit,* Neue Ansätze für Design und Ökologie in der Möbelindustrie, ProÖko Servicegesellschaft ökologischer Einrichtungshäuser mbH, Workshop on Agritechnica, Hannover, 2001.
[54] Cp. *FINANZtest Magazin* (Ed.), Grüne Geldanlage: Die Guten, in: FINANZtest, 2007, Magazine No. 2, p. 24 et seqq.
[55] Cp. *FINANZtest Magazin* (Ed.), Grüne Gewinne, in: FINANZtest, 2006, Magazine No. 6, p.39 et seq.

German business *Eco-Express GmbH* conducts launderettes which are equipped with eco efficient machines. Summarising the number of possibilities in which sustainable products or services may be offered are various. Many niche markets offer sustainable products and the future will show off which products are accepted by consumers and thus penetrate the commodity market.

5 Environmental aware and social responsible business

History shows that companies which refused environmental protection and reacted more on legislative regulations missed dramatic market potentials and innovation chances. A proactive behaviour in the field of environmental protection and social responsibility is thus needed to create first mover advantages.

In the beginning of the 1990ies the concept of sustainability appeared, expressing basically the considerateness on society, ecology and economy. The idea motivates companies to regard environmental and social undertakings equally and comprehend it as a chance for economic benefits. Moreover sustainability gets an integral part on the normative management level and a popular communication tool for environmental and social considerateness of corporate philosophy. Why and to which extent is explained in the subsequent chapter.

Indeed non-governmental organisations respectively consumers can animate a business to rethink. A *Weber Shandwick* survey from the year 2001 indicates that among 8000 high-education/high-income consumers nearly 80% of the people in the USA have considered switching brands when a company was negatively portrayed in the media in respect of social responsibility issues. Equivalent figures for European countries ranged from Germany with 75%, to the UK with 66%, and Italy lagging with 42%.[56] In this way the sportswear company *Nike* faced the influence of consumers at the end of the 1990ies. Different non-governmental organisations discovered various violations of human rights and inhuman working conditions in Asian *Nike* factories and published these exposures. The negative press provoked a distinctive decrease of sales figures in western countries. *Nike* thereupon joined the *Fair Labour Association* and established a department for Corporate Social Responsibility (CSR).

---

[56] Cp. *WBCSD* (Ed.), Driving Success - Marketing and Sustainable Development, 2005, available online www.wbscd.org, l.c. p. 4

Nevertheless there are examples in which environmental or social considerateness is integrated into the mission statement from the inside of a business. In spite of a difficult industry surrounding the mail-order business *Otto* is pushed persistently by one entrepreneurial personality into the direction of sustainable value chains, product development and market acceptance[57] as outlined in chapter 5.2.1.

Further public pressure goes back to business rankings which analyse environmental and social awareness. *Globally Corporate Knights Inc.* and *Innovest Strategic Value Advisors Inc.* published a list of the hundred most sustainable corporations in 2005. Therein companies which are listed in the *MSCI* World are selected in terms of their sector specific environmental, social and governance risks and opportunities. Thus companies are compared to their peers to evaluate the best in class.[58]

Such a ranking has always an indirect influence on the image of the company in public. In either case enterprises aim on being named in the field of the best rated business. Because the environmental and social image of a company is said to influence the total revenue, profitability and sourcing of qualified employees. However it needs to be considered who imposes a ranking, whether an institute or the media e.g. learned journals. In public discussions rankings popularise an appropriate instrument to create stress in competition among enterprises of one industry. They also activate the process of rethinking from an outside point of view.
Meanwhile businesses recognized the advantages of such studies and often use the results to detect weaknesses. In Germany for example the *Hamburger Environmental Institute (HUI)* publishes a ranking of the 50 most sustainable chemical- and pharmaceutical businesses. *Henkel* which was rated only as sufficient in the field of eco sponsoring in the year 1996 used this study to raise additional funds and could thus proceed to a good valuation in 1999.[59]

---

[57] Cp. *Schaltegger, Stefan,* in: Nachhaltiges Wirtschaften, Handelsblatt, 12. Juni 2006
[58] Cp. *Corporate Knights Inc.*, Karen Kun (Ed.), Toronto, 14.01.2007, available online www.global100.org
[59] Cp. *Palass, Brigitta,* Chemische Reinigung, in: Manager Magazin, 1999, Magazine Nr. 9, P. 136

5.1 Motivations

After outlining external pressures the question remains which internal reasons arise from including sustainability into a business mission statement and thereby the question is put: 'does it pay to be green or social?'.

Schmidheiny developed in *Changing Course* the instrument of eco efficiency which became allegory for the linkage of environmental protection and economic benefits. The concept of eco efficiency is applied in production, mainly by using the key word 'cleaner production'. The approach indicates resource efficiency by optimising the complete production process. Thereby the focus is on recovering by-products and on reusing waste, which in return saves cost. Investing in innovations is as well a part of this approach. Finally a new design of processes, technologies and products enables a competitive advantage. By promoting innovations which do not only comply with law but exceed regulations policy can be influenced to co-initiate a new regulation.[60] Pioneer companies are thus given first mover advantages.

Whereas the environmental aspects deliver economic justified reasons, social aspects and their benefit is questionable. *Adidas* which ran a trustworthy sustainability programme experienced the advantages of a good corporate citizenship in 1998. The press' discovery that prisoners of war were employed for producing footballs for the World Cup in 1998 provoked no greater profit loss. Consequently the cases of *Nike* (see chapter 5) and *Adidas* show that social aspects need to be considered as soft value adders and as a prophylactic measure. The essential advantage of a company that engages in social affairs lies in the creation of a positive long-term image which is easier to regenerate in the case of an upcoming scandal.[61]

Consequently environmental undertakings lead to economic, social actions lead to image improvements. *Hardtke* names next to the classic factors cost-saving and image improvement following advantages for a business:

---

[60] Cp. *Hardtke, Arnd; Prehn, Marco* (Ed.), Perspektiven der Nachhaltigkeit, Vom Leitbild zur Erfolgsstrategie, Betriebswirtschaftlicher Verlag Dr. Th. Gabler GmbH, Wiesbaden, 2001, p.65
[61] Cp. Ibid., p. 218 et seq.

- Increase of profit by implementation of measures before production starts or before a product/service is placed on market,
- Quality of products and services by improvement of single attributes quality increases and costs are reduced,
- Principle of precaution by extension of compliance to law, political influence can be exercised and flexibility towards new developments on markets, in society or in policy can be established.
- Risk management by valuing of sustainable actions as additive in risk management investors can provide new capital,
- Employees by increasing value of the image in public new and qualified employees can be employed respectively kept.
- Loyalty and customer retention by involving environmental and social responsibility into purchase decisions new customers can be acquired and customers' loyalty can be maintained.[62]

Here the 'chicken and egg question' raises: Are sustainable oriented enterprises economically successful or do economic successful enterprises act more sustainable? Many surveys analysed the connection of sustainable orientation and economic success. Some studies agree that ecological responsible enterprises perform as well economically successful respectively agree with the result of the comparison between the stock index: the business *Sustainability Asset Management* (*SAM*) compared the stock quotation of the six leading chemical business with six environmental passive companies between 1994 and 1999. During five years a growth of 300% could be watched by the pioneers. In contrast passive enterprises gained a growth of 200%. Based on the indicators *SAM* developed in co-operation with *Dow Jones* a separate sustainability index. 236 enterprises out of 3000 *Dow Jones* participators could be registered in *Dow Jones Group Sustainability Index* (*DJGSI*). Since its introduction *DJGSI* shows in comparison to stock index *MSCI World* a better performance.[63]

There are studies which testify a neutral or a negative context, but *Margolis & Walsh* compared 127 studies about the context of 'corporate social and financial performance' from 1972 till 2002. Almost half of the studies (54) detected a positive

---

[62] Cp. Ibid., p. 70 et seqq.
[63] Cp. *Hardtke, Arnd; Prehn, Marco* (Ed.), Perspektiven der Nachhaltigkeit, Vom Leitbild zur Erfolgsstrategie, Betriebswirtschaftlicher Verlag Dr. Th. Gabler GmbH, Wiesbaden, 2001, p. 79

context, seven studies a negative, 20 studies a mixed and only 28 studies could determine no correlation.[64]

5.2 Implementation of sustainability

In companies sustainable targets are anchored with different priorities. Thereby the range is determined on the one hand by legislative regulations or norms. On the other hand it is determined by the acceptation of ecological and social responsibility. Business which want to install sustainable marketing need to bring ecological, economic and social targets in line. By using sustainable arguments (e.g. in advertising) without revealing competence in corresponding problem solving (e.g. no sustainable adaptation of production processes and technologies) a lack of credibility emerges from the stakeholders' point of view. A business thereby risks its legitimacy and its competitive position.[65] Sustainable marketing needs to be integrated into the whole management concept of a business, which results in an integral consideration of all functional units for planning and tasking.

The triple bottom line approach is currently one of the most established concepts for corporate sustainability. It refers to the column approach of sustainable development and builds up three focus points for sustainable oriented marketing management. Thereby the author *Zadek* subdivides a companies' structure into three levels with respect to:

- Corporate vision and policy on the normative level: They comprise mission statement and principles, which serve for orientation of management and employees throughout the organisation. They determine the value system and the corporate culture.

- Strategies of the enterprise respectively of the business units on the strategic level: Strategies and objectives, which should secure success and the reputation of the enterprise medium to long-term. Here one can differ between market, financial, environmental and social strategies.

---

[64] Cp. *Margolis, Joshua D., Walsh, James P.,* Misery Loves Companies: Rethinking Social Initiatives by Business, In: Administrative Science Quarterly Vol. 48 (2003), p. 268-305
[65] Cp. *Balderjahn, Ingo,* Nachhaltiges Marketing-Management, Lucius&Lucius Verlagsgesellschaft mbH, Stuttgart, 2004, p. 58 et seqq.

- Structure, processes and activities of the enterprise or one of its business units on the operational level: One the one hand these are the applied measures and investments for implementation of the strategy as well as management and controlling systems. On the other hand they also comprise the company organisation structure and the process organisation.[66]

The following describes in detail two possibilities to integrate the claim of corporate sustainability. In scope of this study the focus is on the implementation of sustainability into the normative level and into the organisational structure.

5.2.1 Sustainability as corporate approach

Experience shows that enterprises are prepared to contribute to solving ecological and social problems. Well-known historic examples range from the council estate of the steel business *Krupp* in Essen to the sports clubs of the chemical business *Bayer*.[67]

In line with the concept of 'sustainable development' nowadays responsibility is transferred to the entrepreneurial level. Thereby one speaks of *Corporate Sustainability* or *Corporate Social Responsibility (CSR)* which refers to a broader context than *Corporate Governance* which comprises the interrelations betweens stockholders or *Corporate Citizenship* which organises the behaviour to societal shareholders.[68]

Corporate Citizenship (CC) is a specific approach which obliges enterprises in the role of a 'good fellow citizen' to contribute responsible to the specific societal surrounding of the enterprise.[69] In scope of this concept companies act usually near their place of business or at their (potential) selling market. Activities in line with *Corporate Citizenship* are not limited to large-scale enterprises; small and medium sized enterprises with a local limited selling market show off social commitment and even connect it to their operational market objective in a higher extent than large-

---

[66] Cp. *Zadek, Simon*, The Civil Corporation: The New Economy of Corporate Citizenship, Earthscan Publications, London, 2001, p. 105 et seq.
[67] Cp. *Hardtke, Arnd; Prehn, Marco* (Ed.), Perspektiven der Nachhaltigkeit, Vom Leitbild zur Erfolgsstrategie, Betriebswirtschaftlicher Verlag Dr. Th. Gabler GmbH, Wiesbaden, 2001, l.c., p. 149
[68] Cp. *Balderjahn, Ingo,* Nachhaltiges Marketing-Management, Lucius&Lucius Verlagsgesellschaft mbH, Stuttgart, 2004 p. 55
[69] Cp. Ibid., p. 53

scale enterprises.[70] In line with the concept of *Corporate Citizenship* enterprises can meet the demands of the intragenerational assumption of responsibility. For example in developing countries access to water, electricity or medicines can be offered by enterprises which therewith have the possibility to prepare or enter the market.

According to the concept of *CSR* enterprises are obliged to responsible behaviour towards employees, society and environment. Besides economic operations social and environmental areas are included. This results in the interaction with markets (e.g. suppliers) and with ecological (e.g. environmental organisation), social (e.g. non profit organisation) and internal shareholders (e.g. employees).[71] Dr. Michael Otto states hereunto that the "*Otto Group* based the corporate philosophy on the principle of sustainability, and as such combined commercial activities with the promotion of ecological and social goals."[72] Corporate Sustainability takes thus place at *Otto group* on the following levels:[73]

- **'Code of Conduct': Responsibility through social standards**
  Regulations towards fair wages, prohibition of child work, discrimination, work safety and working times are set by the Code of Conduct and correspondingly evaluated, especially for suppliers' occupied employees.
- **'Pure-Wear': Responsibility towards customers**
  Otto developed with partners organic cotton textiles with an adequate ecological oriented raw material production and a social acceptable processing along the value chain.
- **'aktiv.net': Responsibility towards employees**
  The project aims on strengthening the awareness of health as well as the perception of societal responsibility at employees.
- **Foundations: Responsibility beyond enterprise**
  The *Michael Otto foundation for environmental protection* focuses on the protection and preservation of water, whereas the *Werner Otto Foundation* aims on supporting medical research in hospitals around its place of business namely Hamburg.
- **'dialogue': Responsibility towards stakeholder**
  Regular reporting aims on networking with relevant stakeholders and emphasize the claim of *Otto* to inspire and to co-operate in the debate of sustainability in the German economy.

---
[70] Cp. Ibid., p. 31
[71] Cp. *Balderjahn, Ingo*, Nachhaltiges Marketing-Management, Lucius&Lucius Verlagsgesellschaft mbH, Stuttgart, 2004, p. 55
[72] Cp. *Otto (GmbH & Co KG)* (Ed.), Brochure Corporate Responsibility at Otto, Hamburg, 2007, p. 3
[73] Cp. Ibid., p. 6 - 28

5.2.2 Sustainability in the organisational structure

Enterprises are required by law to consign representatives which are authorised to manage distinct tasks in the area of environmental protection. Tasks of these representatives can range from the observation of law to the exertion of influence on environmental sound process design. Additional representatives' tasks can be extended to informing of employees or reporting of management. Special concepts are set up for managing sustainability throughout the organisation. For example functional organisations can install a department for environmental affairs or an administrative position. Matrix organisations can introduce environmental protection as cross functional task. Project organisations are best to set up 'environmental protection teams'.[74] However "one needs to caution against the perception of ecology as new subject for experts, which absolves the remainder of executives and employees from thinking and acting in ecological categories."[75]

Besides the legislative policy of each state a variety of volunteer international agreements exist which are concretised as objectives, guidelines or standards to encourage sustainable management. For environmental protection three audit concepts established: *British Standard (BS) 7750, EMAS* and *ISO 14001*. Few years ago enterprises hesitated to allow inspection for certification. Today these certificates are considered as state of the art. In alliance to environmental management systems I would like to point at social management systems. These aim at establishing and developing social responsible actions in business.

The mail-order business *OTTO Group* holds its pioneer role through the implementation of an integral environmental- and social management system to realize the vision of sustainability. Thereby the social system is based on and linked to the environmental management system (cp. figure 5-1).
The executives determine the environmental policy and the code of conduct. By means of the code of conduct the managers need to elaborate the environmental strategies. Teams of the operational level apply these strategies in practice. For optimising this system the team consists of managers from different areas such as

---

[74] Cp. *Balderjahn, Ingo,* Nachhaltiges Marketing-Management, Lucius&Lucius Verlagsgesellschaft mbH, Stuttgart, 2004, p. 45
[75] Cp. *Ulrich, Hans*, Systemorientiertes Management: das Werk von Hans Ulrich, Haupt Verlag, Bern/Stuttgart/Wien, 2001, l.c., p. 328

purchase/ administration, marketing/sales, production/technology. This should secure the integration of decision-makers and persons from all operational areas who are affected by planning and implementing product- and business related environmental and social measures. Additional support is given by the department of 'Corporate Responsibility'. Its tasks includes the enhancement of the system, the nomination of responsibilities, the documentation of processes as well as the general communication.

Figure 5-1: Environmental and social management system at Otto

Corporate Vision: Sustainability	
Environmental management system	Social management system
Environmental policy	Social policy
Environmental directed strategies	Social directed strategies
Environmental programmes and measures	Social programmes and measures
Internal Environmenttal and social report/ External sustainability report	
Integrated environmental and social management system	

Source: translated acc. to *Balderjahn, Ingo*, l.c., p. 214

Initiatives, concepts and standards are additional instruments for transferring environmental and social responsibility throughout an organisation. Mentionable is on the one hand the initiative *'Responsible Care'* which was established by the chemical industry. It stands for the willingness of continuous improvement of safety, health and environmental protection, independent from statutory provisions. On the other hand the *'Global Compact'* was set up in order to comprise *'Codes of Conduct'*. Thereby the *Compact* claims from its members to respect human rights, keep to basic labour legislation, protect environment and to oppose all kinds of corruption in public.

Executives of the chemical enterprise *Henkel* decided to join the *Global Compact* in 2003. Internally *Henkel* connects the nine principles of the *Global Compact* to the *Safety, Health, Environment (SHE) management system*. Thereby the social parameters from the *Global Compact* complete the guidelines of *SHE* to form the

'Code of Corporate Sustainability' which reveals the business' principles for sustainable management.[76]

The Code serves as a purchasing guideline which gets completed by business specific quality specifications. Suppliers and service providers are thus evaluated in terms of the *SHE* regulations and in terms of the *Global Compact* principles, such as quality, human rights, employee standards and anti-corruption.

In line with the *Product Stewardship* employees of product development and application technology consult the experts from the department of 'Corporate Safety'. Criteria of product responsibility throughout the life cycle are therein discussed. In co-operation with the 'Sustainable Council' global product development and marketing allocate criteria to single products for a sustainable oriented marketing (see also figure 5-2).[77] Subsequently strategies are developed to communicate the ecological and social arguments to public.

Environment, quality and social responsibility are consquently linked at *Henkel* directly. And the all-embracing quality orientation contributes to the sustainable orientation.

Figure 5-2: Product Responsibility at Henkel

Source: translated acc. to. *Henkel KGaA* (2006), l.c., p. 14

---

[76] Cp. *Henkel KGaA* (Ed.), Nachhaltigkeitsbericht 2005, Düsseldorf, 2006, p. 4
[77] Cp. *Henkel KGaA* (Ed.), Nachhaltigkeitsbericht 2005, Düsseldorf, 2006, p. 5

5.3 Communication

Do good and talk about it, or at least get others to talk about it. In fact media and internet exert influence on the image of business. In return on the one hand corporate communication needs to present positive activities of an organisation. On the other hand corporate communication needs to build up a basis to prevent negative public attention.[78] In line many enterprises start to communicate their environmental and social activities of their mission and their policy in advertisements. Thereby many campaigns are characterised by a unqiue metaphor in reference to the enterprise. For example the German business *Esso AG* (subsidiary of the American *Exxon Corporation*) promotes since 1920 the tiger as 'symbol for power and energy' and supports the preservation of the threatened species.[79]

In 2000 the power company *British Petroleum (BP)* created a new image. The initials *BP* should stand from then on for 'Beyond Petroleum'. Parallel the well-known logo was substituted by a new corporate design, namely the *BP* flower.[80] The chemical corporation *Dupont* promotes itself as an 'earth science pioneer' by making propositions for environmental and social protection on a 'to do list for the planet'. The service provider *MasterCard* differs in line with the 'priceless campaign' the brand of *Mastercard* with the following expressing core brand message: 'there are some things that money can't buy – for everything else there is mastercard'. Whereas the brands such as *Amex* and *Visa* stand for materialsm and a wealthy lifestyle *Mastercard* communicates responsible attitudes towards the consumers' spending as well as an indirect endorsement of a more sustainable consumption.[81]

By setting up of a rather emotional related campaign the retail business *Otto* promotes its environmental responsibility currently. Thereby the slogan 'Look good – feel good' should communicate *Otto*s' new 'Season for comfortable feeling: eudermic spring fashion'. Such advertising slogans do not just animate consumers; slogans of

---

[78] Cp. *Hardtke, Arnd; Prehn, Marco* (Ed.), Perspektiven der Nachhaltigkeit, Vom Leitbild zur Erfolgsstrategie, Betriebswirtschaftlicher Verlag Dr. Th. Gabler GmbH, Wiesbaden, 2001, p. 217
[79] Cp. *Bunk, Burkhardt*, Corporate Citizenship und Marketing: Wie Synergien erschlossen werden, in: Absatzwirtschaft, 10/ 2003, p. 26 et seq.
[80] Cp. Ibid., p. 35
[81] Cp. *McCann-Erickson / UNEP* (Ed.), Brochure Can sustainability sell?, Paris, First Edition, 2002, p. 24

this kind attribute the success of a campaign to the advertising business as well as to its sustainable thinking competitors.

However campaigns do not necessary lead to success, sometimes they turn to a flop. The conflict of the enterprise *Shell* and the sinking of the oil platform *Brent Spar* in the year 1995 serves here as an excellent example: before sinking the platform *Shell* started a print campaign in which the organisation confessed itself to 'special responsibility' for society and environment.[82] Thereby *Shell* forgot that the act of sinking a oil-rig had a higher information value than statements of the campaign. Actions are thus a communication tool and in extreme situations they can thwart other communication efforts.

In contrast a good example can be given by *Toyota* which ran the global corporate communication campaign 'aim: zero emissions' to associate its brand image with eco-friendly technologies. At the same time *Toyota* started its *Prius* campaign in Japan just a couple of months before the signature of the Kyoto protocol. In the United States it coincided with the "Anti - *Sport Utility Vehicles (SUV)* - Campaign" and a debate on emission standards. That allowed *Prius* to benefit from fiscal and legal incentives such as the use of the car pool lane by single occupant hybrid vehicles in California, as well as from an unsolicited support from celebrities.[83]

Social awareness is communicated to an increasing amount by activtities of a business. Here social initiatives serve as transmitter for communication. However the headlines of the fashion company *American Apparels'* will probably be remembered. Slogans as 'Fuck the brands that are fucking the people' or 'Sweatshop-free T-shirts™ Made in Los Angeles' are combined with racy pictures of people from the street, employees and even the executive *Dov Charney* himself. The rethink process is here as well communicated indirectly.[84]

Corporate reporting on non-financial issues is becoming a standard practice among large companies since the *EU Eco Audit* regulation of 1996 claims to publish ecological goals and measures in form of environmental reports.[85] However sustainability reports should not simply consist of an environmental report which

---

[82] Cp. *Klaus, Elisabeth*, Öffentlichkeit als Sebstverständigungsprozess, Das Beispiel Brent Spar, in: *Röttger, Ulrike*, PR Kampagnen: Über die Inszenierung von Öffentlichkeit, VS Verlag für Sozialwissenschaften, Wiesbaden, 3. rev. Ed.., 2006, p. 51 et seq.
[83] Cp. UNEP (Ed.), Brochure: Talk the walk – advancing sustainable lifestyles through Marketing and Communications, Nairobi, Kenya, 2005, p. 34
[84] Cp. Ibid., p. 22
[85] Cp. *Balderjahn, Ingo,* Nachhaltiges Marketing-Management, Lucius&Lucius Verlagsgesellschaft mbH, Stuttgart, 2004, p. 57

integrates a social section. Moreover the focus herein needs to be on ecologic, social and economic topics. The guidelines made by the *Global Reporting Initiative* currently form the most significant framework for public reporting. They aim at creating a standard to compare enterprises' values respectively principles such as trustworthiness and consistency. The structure of a report is kept very tight and e.g. statements of the executives, a description of the organisation profile and the business policy as well as the result of operations. Additionally criteria should also refer to qualitative areas like management systems, stakeholder relationships and product performances. Thereby present and future business performance should be regarded equally. At this point some suggestions are given for topics that may be communicated in a report:

- ecological aspects: influences of processes, products and services on emissions, usage of natural resources and considerateness on human health.
- social aspects: relationships to employees, co-operations with customers, suppliers, investors and partners, treatment of minorities, women and children; involvement of regional, national or international societal topics or policy.
- economic aspects: financial performance, extended to activities which create product and service demand, payment of employees, contribution to local social environment.[86]

Until now sustainable reporting is still in its infancy. It remains open if sustainability reports are accepted as communication tool in line with marketing and at public relation departments. Or whether enterprises will prefer other instruments of marketing such as advertisement, sponsoring or design for environment, which will be explained in Chapter 7. At the end of this chapter I would like to quote *Dr. Wissler*, chairman of *Novartis* Germany which claims that "trust of public in organisational action is nowadays an economic value of rising importance".[87] A true and faithful implementation of sustainable values in line with eco-marketing will pay off for entperprises and besides will be worth for the ecological respectively for the social environment.

---

[86] Cp. *Hardtke, Arnd; Prehn, Marco* (Ed.), Perspektiven der Nachhaltigkeit, Vom Leitbild zur Erfolgsstrategie, Betriebswirtschaftlicher Verlag Dr. Th. Gabler GmbH, Wiesbaden, 2001, p. 232
[87] Cp. Ibid, l.c., p. 220

6 Formulation of strategic marketing in relation to sustainability

Sustainable strategies are medium to long-term formulated decisions of general principle necessary for the implementation of sustainability as a role model. Thereby elements of sustainability need to be included in a business' vision, in the detailed implementation of single measures and in the establishment of a continuous learning process. It is not sufficient to launch measures and projects which do not originate a superior strategy. To realize economic, ecologic and social business objectives sustainability has to be initiated and controlled by top management.

Until today there is no success story or a scheme with a 'how to...' in order to approach sustainability strategically and operatively. Each business needs to formulate its own view of sustainability, as well as it needs to determine the relevance and the handling of the topic. In context *Arthur D. Little* states that "sustainable management aims at a reciprocal adaptation and optimisation of the business value, environmental performance and societal responsibility in strategy and its implementation – at present and for future."[88]

6.1 Business types

Strategies in marketing deal with decisions of general principle in business. They serve as direction giving orientation and as an approach for the operational marketing instruments. At the same time they present suitable application possibilities for the instruments and determine options for successful strategic directions. This includes the determination of strategic business sectors and strategies towards market participants.

In general one assumes a two dimensional market behaviour. On the one hand a customer oriented, on the other hand a competitive behaviour. If focus is on a customer oriented behaviour, one determines the degree of differentiation between specific customer clusters and adjusts the strategy. The competitive approach envisions – mainly through the publications of Michael Porter regarding the topic of competitive strategies – three basic strategic concepts: quality respectively differentiation strategy, cost respectively price leadership, concentration strategy on possible market niches, details hereunto in chapter 6.2.

---

[88] Cp. Ibid., p. 97 et seq.

Before formulating objectives enterprises should be aware of their environmental as well as social positioning. In scope with the examination of 195 German enterprises *Hahn* and *Scheermesser* detected three basic positions: sustainability leaders (ca. 25%), environmental followers (ca. 42%) and traditionalists (ca. 33%).

Sustainable leaders are characterised by the implementation of sustainable instruments and a systematic involvement of social aspects. Environmental followers are characterised by the appliance of environmental management systems. It is assumed that those businesses will move towards sustainability in long-term. Traditionalists adhere to *Milton Friedmans* 'the business of business is business' and only adapt the topic for external presentation of the company.[89] Beyond *Hardtke* describes five general business types which build the base of operations:

1.) **Introverted type**
activities are considered but only included sporadically or in compliance to legislation; they move within the mass and react when requirements became standard according to the wait and see approach.

2.) **Extroverted type**
activities are directed towards environment and society in compliance to stakeholders, many environmental programmes can be found although significant changes are missing.

3.) **Conservative type**
activities are carried out in alliance to cost leadership, competitive advantage is achieved by innovation such as material and resource efficiency (eco efficiency), the true dimension of sustainability remains thereby untouched.

4.) **Visionary type**
activities are here included as core characteristic in the strategy, by dealing with the topic sustainability new approaches evolve and product to service solutions are created which offer extreme competitive advantage for consumers.

5.) **Transforming type**
activities are based on re-engineering of the organisation as a whole and the consecutive rebuilding based on sustainable development. Thereby characteristics of extroverted, conservative and visionary are integrated to the same extent and their specific leverages are used to build new markets.[90]

---

[89] Cp. *Hahn, Tobias; Scheermesser, Mandy*, Das Nachhaltigkeitsengagement deutscher Unternehmen, in: UmweltWirtschaftsForum UWF, 02/2005, p. 70-75
[90] Cp. *Hardtke, Arnd; Prehn, Marco* (Ed.), Perspektiven der Nachhaltigkeit, Vom Leitbild zur Erfolgsstrategie, Betriebswirtschaftlicher Verlag Dr. Th. Gabler GmbH, Wiesbaden, 2001, p. 98 et seq.

In alliance of analysing the sustainable situation in a business, it is necessary to deal with the basic positioning on the target market. Competitors are mainly found on various levels which results in a classification of four possible positions: market leader holding a market share of ca. 40%, a market challenger holding ca. 30%, a market follower trying to keep its share of ca. 20% and a market nicher which shares the amount of 10% with other niche occupants.[91] Thus after a business is aware of its position and that of its main competitors as well as of its own sustainable compatibility it can begin with creating special sustainable oriented marketing strategies.

6.2 Sustainable oriented competitive strategies

Different paths of enterprises can be detected according to the corporate philosophy and the role of decision makers. Basically strategic approaches can be carried out in a defensive as well as in an offensive way. Defensive behaviour is mostly considered as risk or as inevitable and hardly as economic or societal chance. Thereby consequences of unsustainable acting are prevailed by strategic withdrawal from environmental harmful business fields or by resisting societal claims. In case of extreme negative consequences defensive behaviour approaches to include parts of sustainability. In contrast offensive strategies concerning sustainability provide competitive advantage and create societal acceptance.[92]

Both strategies are applied to assure the continuance of an enterprise. Followed firstly by the detection that sustainable management beholds the possibility to save costs. And followed secondly by the identification of the great potential of sustainable oriented product differentiation. This connects to the business' discovery when introducing innovative products in markets that the general framework of policy and/or societal surrounding needs to be changed, in order to be successful with socio-ecological products in mass market.[93] In alliance to this thread *Dyllick* enhanced *Porters*' basic types for competitive strategies to five sustainable oriented

---

[91] Cp. *Kotler, Philip; Bliemel, Friedhelm*, Marketing-Management, Schäffer-Poeschel Verlag, Stuttgart, 8. rev. Ed, l.c., p. 597
[92] Cp. *Balderjahn, Ingo*, Nachhaltiges Marketing-Management, Lucius&Lucius Verlagsgesellschaft mbH, Stuttgart, 2004, p.101
[93] Cp. *Dyllick, Thomas*, Nachhaltigkeitsorientierte Wettbewerbsstrategien, in: *Linne, Gudrun, Schwarz, Michael* (Ed.), Handbuch Nachhaltige Entwicklung: Wie ist nachhaltiges Wirtschaften machbar?, Verlag Leske + Budrich, Opladen, 2003, p. 267-271

competitive strategies. Thereby the business types set up in chapter 6 are attributed specific benefits on which the strategy type is based (cp. table 6-1).

Cost or quality aware strategies are thereby for enterprises not new. In the last decade new efficient instruments were applied for cost reduction or for quality improvement. A reduction of machines or material costs is from the sustainable point of view not wrong. Thus a reduction of applied resources or a reduction of costs through environmental integrated process measures can result in economic as well as in ecological advantages. Next to better quality products and higher turnovers quality audits or quality management may help to develop ecological acceptable product attributes such as longer product lifetime or easy disposal.

Important for the success is besides the pre-given sustainable awareness and a corresponding trustworthy sustainable strategy also the awareness of the target groups' consumption behaviour. Market success will not be generated without meeting the needs of customers e.g. textiles demand the right colour and shape. Thus the role of an innovative business is combined with the implementation of a professional marketing which considers the dimensions of sustainability. Through targeted changes of products and through a proactive and trustworthy communication policy in line with price and promotional measures business can differentiate the added value of social and ecological acceptable products respectively services and therewith gain competitive advantage.

However enterprises are offered a new competitive chance to gain besides a cost and innovation leadership as well a proactive role in the pathway to sustainable development. Under the keyword 'improve market framework conditions' the *World Business Council for Sustainable Development* (*WBCSD*) suggests to influence as well legislative regulations, because education of consumers e.g. in questions of energy consumption is often not sufficient.[94] The same is valid for production in which political changes may help to e.g. cut down ecological disadvantageous subventions. Thus the trend of renewable energies in Germany at the end of 1990ies could not developed without a corresponding regulation about the uptake of green power.

---

[94] Cp. *WBCSD* (Ed.), Brochure: Sustainability through the market. Seien kess to Success, 2001, available online www.wbcsd.org, p. 18

Table 6-1: Sustainable competitive strategies

Type	Goals	Implementation	Consequences
1. Minimisation respectively control of risks: Safe type	Reduction of risks and fulfilment of stakeholders' claims	Risk management in line with environmental management systems, e.g. ISO 14001 and EMAS or financial audits	If passive introduction: image of late mover may occur. Active behaviour enables the basis for progressing competitive sustainable strategies
2. Improvement of image and reputation: Authentic type	Prevention of reputation harm respectively building up of values and image	Risk management and communication management in line with corporate identity	Image for employees, society, finance market. Enables a positive design of stakeholders' relations
3. Improvement of productivity and efficiency: Cost type	Eco efficiency respectively socio efficiency for a win-win potential	Reduction of costs, environmental harm per product unit thereby end of pipe technology must be included into all operational processes. Moreover socio efficiency enables the increase of employees and partners performance by involvement of social concerns	Sustainable cost reduction can be met which reduces social disburdens (e.g. internal: organisational development which leads to efficient processes and satisfied employees, external: subventions for business locations in economic weak regions)
4. Differentiation on market: Innovative type	price between niche and mass market, communication should aim on consumption not on renouncement, involvement of public and policy	Research and development throughout products' life cycle thereby focus on innovation, design for environment.	Satisfaction of the relevant customer needs, thereby professional marketing besides eco and sustainability oriented marketing for successful product resp. service placement
5. Development of markets: Transformative type respectively Proactive leader	Involvement in the structural change of economy and society	Lobbyism for sustainable challenges measures (e.g. CO2 tax) and Public Relation, thereby involvement in the set up of industry standards and labels (e.g. FSC) or commitment in the general framework (e.g. GRI for sustainability reporting)	Insecure Investment

Source: compiled by the author, based on *Dyllick, Thomas*, l.c. p. 267-271

6.3 Planning instruments of strategic marketing

Strategic decisions are made in scope of marketing by means of various instruments. On the one hand decision making considers threats and opportunities of market related, technological and social requirements in the macroenvironmental context. On the other hand microenvironment related decisions are mainly determined by strengths and weaknesses which direct the reaction on ecological and social challenges. Known strategic and operative planning methods of environmental management comprise the SWOT analysis as well as the value chain analysis.

In context of this study only external planning instruments should be examined. Among special methods which range from the scenario technique, cross-impact analyse to the issue analyse[95] I would like to introduce the portfolio analysis. Basically a portfolio analysis is based on separation and classification of strategic business units in a two-dimensional room. The popular market-share/ market-growth portfolio of the *Boston Consulting Group (BCG)* serves as basic concept. Therein the market growth is opposed to the relative market share in a matrix of four fields. In order to determine the ecological strategic position products respectively product lines or whole strategic business units are considered in dependency of "relative advantages of ecological behaviour (improvement of profit, market share and image related to main competitor) and environmental endangerment (results from sourcing, production, usage and disposal of the product)."[96] In figure 6-1 an example is given for an ecological portfolio developed by *Sturm*. Here the size of the circles corresponds to the ecological impact of the annual sales volume.

At this place a portfolio analysis should be exemplified by means of the matrix of *BASF* which puts the environmental impact in relation to the customer value. Thereby the total costs from the customers point of view are visualised on the horizontal axis. The vertical axis describes the overall environmental harm of a system or a product. The outcome of this is a four quadrant scheme. Products situated on the right top quadrant dispose at the same time low environmental impact and low costs. These products or systems are described as eco efficient. In contrast products situated on

---

[95] Cp. *Balderjahn, Ingo*, Nachhaltiges Marketing-Management, Lucius&Lucius Verlagsgesellschaft mbH, Stuttgart, 2004, l.c. p. 80 et seqq.
[96] Cp. *Meffert, Heribert; Kirchgeorg, Manfred*, Marktorientiertes Umweltmanagement, Schäffer Poeschel Verlag, Stuttgart, 3. rev. Ed., 1998, l.c., p. 157

the left bottom quadrant cause high costs and dispose about high environmental impact. These products are judged as less eco efficient.[97] By means of the distance from the diagonal line a measurement for the eco efficiency can thus be given. Consequently products can be identified easily in terms of environmental friendliness and economic sustainability.

In line with sustainability an appropriate portfolio method is needed to determine the evaluation and positioning for products, technologies or strategic business units. Thereby the portfolio analysis provides a useful, compressed and structured visual impression of the sustainable situation of single business divisions. Evaluation and positioning are based on the performance (business internal dimension) and on the contributions to markets, environment and society (business external dimension). The description of the analyse units (e.g. product) takes place within a matrix defined for the dimensions of market, environment and society (cp. figure 6-3). The size of the cycle serves thereby as measurement for the significance e.g. of the product for the business (e.g. contribution to turnover). For each analysing unit a position on the three dimensions is defined. Therefore scoring models can be applied. It is as well possible to evaluate and position an analysing unit in a matrix along the three dimension (cp. figure 6-4).[98]

Figure 6-1: Example for an impact/profitability portfolio

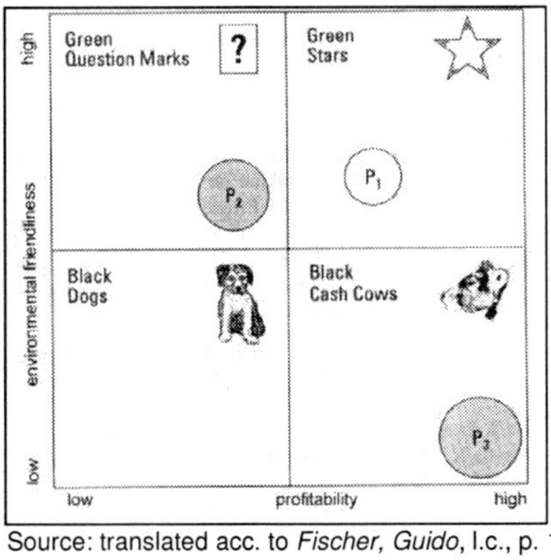

Source: translated acc. to *Fischer, Guido,* l.c., p. 107

---

[97] Cp. *Kicherer, Andreas et al.,* Ökoeffizienz Analyse „made by BASF" verspricht eine mehrfache Rendite, in: *BASF AG* (Ed), Speech on Envitec "Von Ökoeffizienz zu nachhaltiger Entwicklung in Unternehmen", Düsseldorf , 15./16.05.01. available online http://corporate.basf.com/en/sustainability
[98] Cp. *Balderjahn, Ingo,* Nachhaltiges Marketing-Management, Lucius&Lucius Verlagsgesellschaft mbH, Stuttgart, 2004, l.c. p. 84 et seqq.

Figure 6-2: Example for an impact/customer value portfolio

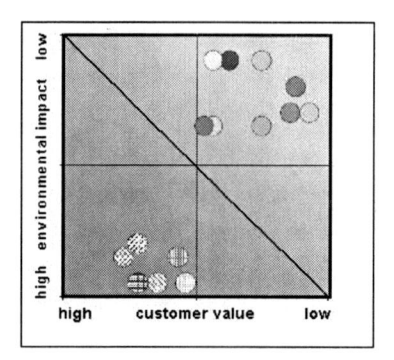

Source: translated acc. *Kicherer, Andreas* et al.

Figure 6-3: Sustainable portfolio for products

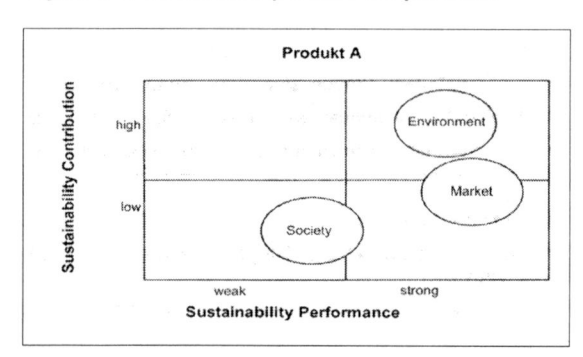

Source: Translated acc. to. *Balderjahn*, l.c., p. 87

Figure 6-4: Twodimensional sustainable portfolio

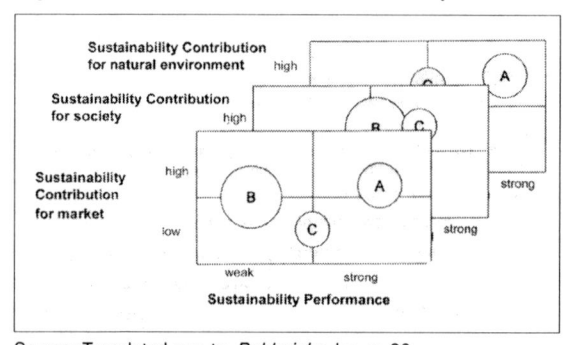

Source: Translated acc. to. *Balderjahn*, l.c., p. 86

7 Instruments of marketing

The implementation of adequate marketing instruments needs to be adapted to the sustainable orientated goal and the market oriented strategy of each business. The ecological orientated marketing mix thereby needs to be considered in detail. It forms the operational part of the marketing strategy and incorporates a choice of ecological relevant instruments. Figure 2-1 shows various modifications of the product-, communications-, distribution- and price policy. Further profound possibilities and extensions should be explained in the following.

7.1 Product political measures

The ecological sound product policy has a significant meaning in ecological oriented marketing, because it comprises all decisive facts which refer to the market-driven design of a business' product mix.[99] Sustainable oriented product policy contains the design of products and services which take criteria of sustainability into account. Sustainable products and services are characterised throughout the entire life cycle – production, distribution, usage and disposal – on the one hand by a lower environmental impact than conventional alternatives of the same product line (environmentally compatible products). On the other hand by a lower exposition of personal or social dangers on humans and their social community (socially acceptable products).[100] In detail social acceptable products are produced under humane working conditions and enable fair trade (e.g. fair trade products such as coffee and tee). Moreover they do not harm health and do not contribute to the burdening of safety systems (e.g. such as cigarette or alcohol consumption).[101]

'Eco design' is the key word for the systematic involvement of environmental- and health aspects throughout the design phase. Therein focus is set on sustainable related product innovation and variation (product improvement and differentiation) as well as on elimination of environmental and social harming products respectively services. Improvements can relate to the core product and its function. Additionally a products' aesthetical (e.g. design), physical and functional (e.g. durability, reliability,

---

[99] Cp. *Meffert, Heribert; Kirchgeorg, Manfred,* Marktorientiertes Umweltmanagement, Schäffer Poeschel Verlag, Stuttgart, 3. rev. Ed., 1998, l.c., p. 285
[100] Cp. *Balderjahn, Ingo,* Nachhaltiges Marketing-Management, Lucius&Lucius Verlagsgesellschaft mbH, Stuttgart, 2004 p. 174
[101] Cp. Ibid., p. 181

application security) and symbolical (e.g. brand name) characteristics can be improved as well as the offered added value (e.g. customer and consulting service). Thereby the requirements of the production process are of specific importance.[102]
A socio-ecological product or service should provide on the one hand an individual added value for consumers in terms of a psychological value by a purer consciousness. On the other hand it should pass on a "basic value in terms of an increase of humans' life quality by improvement of the environmental and social value".[103]

The quality profile therefore needs to balance between the added value and the perceived customer value. Therein one should aim at satisfying the quality demands of the target group and at the same time reach a plus in environmental compatibility in important ecological dimensions.

For evaluation and weighting of the environmental and social consequences in the single product life cycle stage following criteria are consultable:

- Production stage   minimal material and energy input,
  implementation of secondary raw material,
  usage of environmental and social harmless materials,
  low pollutant emissions,
  low variety of materials and abondonment of composites,
  labelling of used materials
- Usage stage   long life by modular design, multiple usage, durability,
  environmental compatible while usage,
  low pollutant emissions,
  safe in application and free of hygienic endangers,
  label
  service by additive service providers, integrated services, substitution services
- Disposal stage   design for recycling, design for disassembly.

Each business which strives for a pro-active, sustainable product management needs to aim at provoking – throughout the whole product life cycle – low ecological and social disadvantages. For penetrating the market with sustainable products the

---
[102] Cp. Ibid., p.180 et seq.
[103] Cp. Ibid., p.177

so called 'cash cows' are the main pillars and are improvable in their ecological and social characteristics, in some ecological dimensions they even perform better than its ecological substitutes.[104]

Actors (such as suppliers, manufacturers, retail) are challenged to accept their responsibility for their produced and marketed product or service. This means health, social and environmental attributes should be considered throughout the value chain of the product and its life cycle in line with the concept of *Product Stewardship* (cp. Chapter 5.2.2, p. 39).[105]

7.1.1 Product responsibility

In the past decade a variety of measures and initiatives were set up to improve products in terms of their environmental impact. The ideas range from design for environment and communicative measures (e.g. labels) up to initiatives of consumer counselling. Since five years a progressing policy is being discussed. *IPP* is the succinct abbreviation for the concept of *'Integrate Product Policy'* which strives for a stronger coherence of various product political measures. Thereby *IPP* schedules on products and services and their ecologic characteristics throughout the whole life cycle. It is targeted on improving their environmental attributes and thereby challenges innovations of products and services.[106]

In business circles this approach faces often mistrust: Does policy interferes with operational product decisions? What is left for business to do?

The implementation of environmental sound resources is just a part of the corporate engagement at *Faber-Castell*. In line with *IPP* the products' whole life cycle is analysed in order to reduce the energy amount to a minimum in the long-run. This includes the choice of raw material and production process, packaging, transport, until the usage of product and its disposal. A checklist enables to consider the life cycle of a single product systematically and measurable.

---

[104] Cp. *Wüstenhagen, Rolf, Villiger, Alex, Meyer, Arnt,* Jenseits der Öko-Nische, Birkhäuser Verlag AG, Basel, 2000, p. 47
[105] Cp. *Balderjahn, Ingo,* Nachhaltiges Marketing-Management, Lucius&Lucius Verlagsgesellschaft mbH, Stuttgart, 2004, p. 177
[106] Cp. *Ministerium für Umwelt und Verkehr Baden-Württemberg* (Ed.), Kooperative Ansätze im Rahmen einer integrierten Produktpolitik, Stuttgart, 2004, p. 5, available online www.uvm.baden-wuerttemberg.de (20.02.2007)

Thus *Faber-Castell* implements for most pencils throughout Europe environmental friendly water based paints. Therefore the production procedure was changed from conventional varnishes with organic solvents to environmental friendly emulsion paints. By this technology *Faber-Castell* could set new standards in the area of pencil varnishing.

In line with the network *COUP 21* the mail-order business *Quelle AG* engages in the project for 'ecological optimisation of the textile value chain', which aims at activating new ecological developments for production, usage and disposal of textiles. Consumer research, supplier standards and qualification of manufacturers contribute to a further ecological improvement of the product range. Thereby the social acceptability of working and production conditions play an increasing role.

The various companies within this study group enabled a wide covering of the *IPP* approach. *Quelle AG* hereby holds its gatekeeper function and thus influences manufacturers and consumers to the same extent. The production oriented aspects of the checklist are helpfully for *Quelle AG* to check internal processes and to adapt the existing instruments to new ecological evaluation possibilities of suppliers. The existing control plans (which integrate aspects of fitness for use, quality and environmental acceptability of products) are in line with the recent 'ecological product analysis' reengineered according to *IPP* criteria. For textiles this study should elicit consumer acceptance of ecological improved clothing as well as it should investigate strategies with which textiles can penetrate the market more efficiently.[107]

7.1.2 Analysis

Because social coherences are complex and ambiguous as well as hard to measure this chapter is limited to ecological efficiency analysis. The significance of environmental protection and the awareness about possible impacts of products on environment resulted in the development of appropriate methods. Meanwhile many instruments exist which strive for an eco efficient design of products and at the same time aim at a reduction of the total consumption of materials and energy. All methods include the analysis of the whole product life cycle 'from cradle to grave', but differ in

---

[107] Cp. *Netzwerk COUP 21* (Ed.), Leitfaden: Management ökologischer Produkte, München, 2001, p.22 et seq., available online www.coup21.de (20.02.2007)

the analysis of the single life cycle steps. Therein the degree of details as well as the number of criteria and considered impact areas varies.[108]

Life Cycle Analysis are planning, information and control instruments for the product policy. One of their tasks is the measuring of product related impacts on environment throughout the whole life 'from cradle to grave'. Other tasks are the preparation and evaluation of results as well as the corresponding presentation. A *Life Cycle Analysis* is thus an instrument for environmental protection as well as for the optimisation of products by comparison to competing products.

A *Life Cycle Analysis* consists of four steps as defined in *ISO 14040* and *14044*: determination of the goal and scope, inventory analysis and impact assessment as well as final interpretation. The *Inventory Analysis* (*LCI*) is an activity for collecting data on inputs (resources and intermediate products) and outputs (emissions, wastes) for all the processes in the product system. The *Impact Assessment* (*LCIA*) translates the inventory data on inputs and outputs into indicators about the product systems' impacts on the environment, on human health, and on the availability of natural resources.

Subsequently the results of the *LCI* and *LCIA* are interpreted according to the goal of the study. Thereby conclusions can be drawn and recommendations can be directed in line with marketing to consumers for further information about the environmental attributes of a product. Often some product managers speak about a 'positive balance' of the product. This statement is not valid, because the interpretation is a comparison between several products as mentioned above, and thus one can only speak of a 'positive balance' compared to the analysis of another product.[109]

The nourishment company *Kraft Jacobs Suchard* developed in co-operation with the *Fraunhofer Institute for process engineering and packaging science* a life cycle analysis for a 1000g package of roasted coffee. The study aimed at identifying areas with critical environmental impact throughout the whole life path, beginning with growing of coffee trees till packaging of coffee beans. Coffee roasting and packaging did not affect the product related result significantly. Moreover areas of coffee cultivation, preparation of green coffee as well as the waste management of the used

---

[108] Cp. *Balderjahn, Ingo,* Nachhaltiges Marketing-Management, Lucius&Lucius Verlagsgesellschaft mbH, Stuttgart, 2004, p. 99
[109] Cp. *European Commission* (Ed.), European Platform on Life Cycle Assessment, Ispra, Italy, 20.02.2007, available online http://lca.jrc.ec.europa.eu/lcainfohub/index.vm

product provoked concretised options for action, which are not suggestible by *Kraft Jacobs Suchard*. Thereby the avoidance of mineral fertilizers through cultivation, dry processing or the usage of thermos flask are possible measures as well as a composting of coffee grounds and filter paper by consumers. Improvements in cultivation as well as information activities towards consumers are advisable measures to change consumption patterns for *Kraft Jacobs Suchard*.[110]

In contrast *Product Line Analyses (PLA)* try to register funcitonal impacts on economy, nature and society throughout the whole life cycle (from raw material, transportation, from production to usage and disposal). Core of this analyse is a matrix, which is consulted to evaluate the particular impacts of certain life cycle stages (horizontal consideration).[111] Social and economic aspects are illustrated and evaluated separately. There are no process regulations respectively standards as in *Life Cycle Analysis*. The ecological part is as state of the art implemented analogue to the process regulations of the life cycle. Subsequently all three parts are evaluated. Besides the integration of social and economic aspects another important difference is the project workshop, in which representatives of all relevant societal groups are involved. So far product line analyses did not established in practice, but in line with sustainable development they will gain in importance.[112]

7.1.3 Packaging policy

In times of rising waste, scarce energy and raw material resources the demands on packaging increase as well. Increased municipal waste creates severe problems for local disposal companies. Packaging, which is considered as accumulative term of various wrapping kinds of one or more products, changed its function due to its marketing meaning. While packaging served mainly as protection during transport it transformed over the years to an important differentiation tool to create competitive advantage. Companies recognized packaging as an interesting promotional tool. Wrappings became more colourful and more informative. Over the time the product could present itself more independently on the point of sale. Packaging became a

---

[110] Cp. *Fraunhofer Institut für Lebensmitteltechnologie und Verpackung*, Vol. 3: Produkt-Ökobilanz vakuumverpackter Röstkaffee, LCA Documents, Eco-Informa Press, Bayreuth, Ed. 1., 1998
[111] Cp. *Balderjahn, Ingo*, Nachhaltiges Marketing-Management, Lucius&Lucius Verlagsgesellschaft mbH, Stuttgart, 2004, p. 99 et seq.
[112] Cp. *Eberle, Ulrike*: Das Nachhaltigkeitszeichen: ein Instrument zur Umsetzung einer nachhaltigen Entwicklung? In: Werkstattreihe Nr. 127, Freiburg: Öko-Institut e.V. Freiburg, 2001, p. 30 et seqq.

distinct element of a branded product, and it needs to be added that it would not be possible to shop in a supermarket without packaging.

The propositions for environmental sound packaging align basically at the aspects of eco design which suggest to:

- consider energy- and material efficiency
  (e.g. such as light weight construction or multi functionality of the product),
- limit or reduce the implementation of harmful material or dangerous substances,
- prefer reusable materials,
- consider durability and long life ability
  (e.g. repairable) ,
- design recyclable or disposable products
  (e.g. low variety of materials and composites) ,
- design the transport environmental friendly
  (e.g. low volume of product respectively packaging).[113]

The ecological as well as economic advantages of the minimisation of packages (e.g. avoidance of secondary packaging and small portion packs) combined with ecological minimum standards persuaded partly in the food industry. Meanwhile it serves retail for prevention of competitive disadvantages as well as for saving costs.
However the packaging design inheres for various products such as cosmetics a high marketing potential. An ecological oriented brand can be better promoted in connection with an environmental sound and innovative package. Also many product managers are aware that creating subjects for "waste" is not longer favourable. The cosmetic and dietary supplement company *Dr. Grandel* optimised its packaging concept. On the one hand they initiated a dual use of outer packaging as transportation cardboard and display for products. On the other hand the new elements such as the implementation of reusable materials, ecological harmless printing inks and avoidance of surface refinement was involved into the existing product development guideline.[114] Such approaches should be state of the art for business as they combine ecological and economical advantages.

---

[113] Cp. *Umweltbundesamt* (ED.), Jahresbericht 2005, p.70 et seqq.
[114] Cp. *Bayerisches Staatsministerium für Umwelt, Gesundheit und Verbraucherschutz* (Ed.), Informationen und Empfehlungen zur integrierten Produktpolitik (IPP) in Marketingkonzepten: Ein Leitfaden von Unternehmen für unternehmen entwickelt, München, 2005, p.31

A forward-looking material for packaging are biodegradable plastics. The polymers of the 'green plastics' can be allocated to their source material, namely starch, sugar, cellulose or synthetic materials. Whether the use of biopolymers will contribute to a more sustainable society is a question that will have to be studied by a representative *Life Cycle Analysis* for each application and by a comparison with existing applications. Representative *LCAs* are needed at material and product levels; they must make allowance for future developments in biopolymers and take account of all relevant environmental impacts associated with the complete product life cycle, including the depletion of raw materials, the agricultural use of fertilizers and pesticides, transportation, utilization and waste disposal.

The environmental benefits of biodegradable packaging must be reflected in cost advantages, if large-scale applications are to become feasible. In the short term, it would be preferable to communicate the functional advantages of biodegradable packaging rather than its ability to compost.

7.1.4 Brand policy

The development and establishment of brands is cost intensive. Consumers are sensitive towards negative headlines of a product, such as scandals at assumed ecological or health harm, revealed child work or inhuman working conditions in a company or at its suppliers. A long term designed brand image can be destroyed in a short time. This results in the corresponding economic consequences such as demand decrease respectively purchasing boycotts. Herein brand policy is of vital importance for protection of the brand.[115] *Balderjahn* detects a brand as sustainable if "it refers to products, which promise respectively guarantee customer a (relative) high environmental- and social acceptability."[116] According to *Balderjahn* a sustainable brand policy includes the following sub-goals, which are complemented by *Meffert* as following:

- Sustainable brands are an essential communication tool towards consumers and a differentiation strategy towards competitors. A brand enables a fast recognition of the product by giving sustainable relevant and creditable product information and marking. (Additionally marking can be implement official respectively certified labels or signets).

---

[115] Cp. *Balderjahn, Ingo*, Nachhaltiges Marketing-Management, Lucius&Lucius Verlagsgesellschaft mbH, Stuttgart, 2004, p.184
[116] Cp. Ibid., p.183

- In foreground is the products' embodiment of an authentic product character, which appears likable on the consumers so that an identification with the product takes place. Thereby brand loyalty is build up, as well as a support for sales is given.
- Brand policy includes the creation of a price political range.
- Maintenance of possibilities for differentiated market development, marking of quality and price advantages towards conventional product variants and implementation of an eco brand as differentiation tool for choosing the distribution channels.

The positive effects can hereby be used for further goods of the product line. The washing powder *Persil* of the company *Henkel* became throughout its history a distinctive brand label. The product became - especially through the favourite "white lady" in the 1920ies - a symbol for clean and brilliant white clothes. This image did not just affect the brand *Persil* but did as well achieve a positive effect on other cleaning agents and detergent product lines. The vision of *Werner & Mertz GmbH* is the maintenance of the natural environment, a careful raw material usage and a sustainable corporate policy.[117] This image can be transmitted by *Frosch*, a brand introduced for detergents besides the established brand *Erdal-Rex*. *Frosch* thereby communicates basically superior cleaning attributes and at the same time protection of human and environment by natural and high performing agents. As 'the most trusted brand' *Frosch* influenced other brands of *Werner & Metz GmbH* such as *tana professional* to which a green product line was added.

Co-branding is another promising possibility to strengthen the sustainable image of a brand. It focuses on the co-operation with a brand of better ecological image. Thereby the brand of the customers' valued component is listed besides the business' own brand, so that both parties can improve their environmental competence. Herefore following variants are possible:

- Involvement of a product component of an environmental brand,
- Creation of additional value by offering service from a successful positioned, environmental oriented service provider,
- Communication of co-operation with an environmental waste management system.[118]

---

[117] Cp. *Werner & Mertz GmbH* (Ed.), Umwelterklärung 2006, Mainz, 2006, p. 4 et seq.
[118] Cp. *Bayerisches Staatsministerium für Umwelt, Gesundheit und Verbraucherschutz* (Ed.), Informationen und Empfehlungen zur integrierten Produktpolitik (IPP) in Marketingkonzepten: Ein Leitfaden von Unternehmen für unternehmen entwickelt, München, 2005, p.57

Co-branding is used for example by the French business *Lafuma group*. Here they initiated a partnership for the brand *Lafuma* with the *Worldwide Fund* (*WWF*). In scope the product line *Lafuma-WWF* was set up.[119]

7.2 Communication policy

Market-oriented sustainable communication informs about eco- and social acceptable products and their production, about sustainable behaviour of a business as well as about further important sustainable facts. Additionally communication needs to practice a dynamic and open dialogue with the business' most important stakeholders such as critics, competitors and consumers.[120] In terms of change from a defensive to a pro-active character enterprises face new challenges in the design of communication. As chapter 5 illustrates, communication gains importance which claims a business to involve communication into their corporate strategy. Thereby the main advantages focus on creating credibility and on building trust to relevant stakeholders (e.g. customers, authorities, shareholders, banks, NGOs) as well as on improving the general image.

Balderjahn understands the term sustainable communication as "the implementation of all communicational instruments of a business for presenting all efforts and prosperities of sustainable development in business".[121] Thereby it could be adjusted to following principles:

a.) *"The aim of communication is the maintenance of credibility in public.* Credibility conditions a clearly visible agreement between words and the effective actions of a company as well as its representatives.

b.) *Communication needs to be personal.* Paper is blush and can hardly transmit trust. Only humans can transmit trust. The actual, provable and visible behaviour of business members is of significance.

---

[119] Cp. *Lafuma* Group (Ed.), Sustainable Development Report Lafuma Group 2005, Anneyron, 2005
[120] Cp. *Hardtke, Arnd; Prehn, Marco* (Ed.), Perspektiven der Nachhaltigkeit, Vom Leitbild zur Erfolgsstrategie, Betriebswirtschaftlicher Verlag Dr. Th. Gabler GmbH, Wiesbaden, 2001, p. 220
[121] Cp. *Balderjahn, Ingo*, Nachhaltiges Marketing-Management, Lucius&Lucius Verlagsgesellschaft mbH, Stuttgart, 2004, p. 187

c.) *Answer the actual put questions.* Instead of the usual dominating company monologues search and develop forms of dialogues in order to avoid answering questions that no one puts while the actual questions are unacknowledged.

d.) *The personal role model of the top management counts.* At the same time it is an illusion to believe that the dialogue could be directed from one position. Rather valid: The more employees can report about environmental activities in public, the more effective and credible is the message. This indicates that each employee is an ambassador of the business.

e.) *Wholeheartedly openness and transparency also in regard to negative aspects.* The reality has always at least two sides: a positive and a negative. The appropriate presentation of the negative is the requirement for accepting the positive.

f.) *No anticipation of decisions.* Communication with public needs transparency of the relevant facts, without willing to anticipate decisions. The one who wants to force decisions seems to be manipulable and loosens its credibility.

g.) *Mass media are the most important bridge to public*, which are available for societal communication, whether or not it suits you. This does not cope with the usual experience that the media is considered as enemy, to whom information is deprived if possible, or to whom - even worse - information is given in small pieces or under enormous pressure. Before communicating with the media one should have done its homework. Facts need to be presented and if possible good documented. The awareness that representatives of the media did their homework incompletely or even worse, does not count as excuse."[122]

The key to success will be a factual information policy which flanks the emotional positioning. This can be achieved by measures of an offensive business reporting, by profound information on the point of sale or via internet, or by combination of a strong brand and an independent accredited eco-label.[123] To implement a successful communication policy following basic instruments are applied:[124]

---

[122] Cp. *Meffert, Heribert*, Marketing: Grundlagen der Absatzpolitik, Gabler-Verlag, Wiesbaden, 7. rev. Ed, 1993, l.c., p. 443
[123] Cp. *Wüstenhagen, Rolf, Villiger, Alex, Meyer, Arnt,* Jenseits der Öko-Nische, Birkhäuser Verlag AG, Basel, 2000, p. 49
[124] Cp. *Engelfried, Justus*, Nachhaltiges Umweltmanagement, Oldenbourg Wissenschaftsverlag GmbH, München, 2004, p.163

Advertising	Advertisements in print, radio, television and cinema broadcast
	Product packaging, package inlet and display material, brochures
	Notepads, magazines, poster, billboards, signs, symbols or logos
	Audiovisual advertising.
Sales promotion	Point-of-sale displays, specialty advertising
	Vending special programmes, competitions, lottery
	Demonstrations, incentives, samples
	Exhibitions, performances, entertainment activities
	Tokens, coupons, rebates, discounts, premiums.
Personal selling	Sales presentations, fairs and trade shows, telephone selling
	Sampling and incentive programmes.
Direct marketing	Catalogues, flyers, mailings, TV-direct, Internet.
Public relations	Press kits, publications, workshops, lectures
	Lobbyism, business reports, sponsoring, care of connection to public.

This list can be extended to sponsoring as well as to dialogue oriented instruments, which all aim at improving the business' image. In line with dialogue oriented instruments public should be integrated into the decision making process of a company, such as choice of location for new headquarters.[125]

In the following paragraphs some communicational instruments should be presented which are close to eco- and socio oriented consumption patterns. However it needs to be reminded that especially for external communication the ecological impact should be taken into account, particularly direct marketing methods have to be considered critically. In terms of television, radio, internet and e-mail the ecological footprint is irrelevant.[126]

7.2.1 Advertising

Consumers have become more interested in the company behind the brand and its values. Yet sustainability takes place on the corporate affairs level as many websites indicate. Therein information on a business' values, responsibilities and their commitment to environment and society is provided. However this does not inform and educate in a pro-active way. These commitments to sustainable development do not contribute to the growth of brand value. More over to strengthen sustainable

---
[125] Cp. Ibid., p. 163
[126] Cp. Ibid., p. 166

development in a business it needs to yield benefits. Advertising can herein help to take the message to their clients and develop as well as defend brand value.[127]

Balderjahn states that a sustainable respectively eco-advertising "targets on the encouragement of sustainable consumption patterns and of purchasing decisions. Besides eco- or social oriented headlines and arguments, brands and labels respectively symbols are applied. It relates to industries (e.g. chemistry), enterprises (e.g. *BASF*) or to products (e.g. dishwasher *AEG* Öko-Favorit)."[128]

Products are often advertised by short formulas such as 'organic', 'eco' or 'natural'. The legal position is determined by the general regulation of the intention to mislead (in Germany according to §3 UWG Act Against Unfair Practices) and by specific regulations of the Foodstuffs and Commodities Act. The *German Advertising Industry* (*ZAW*) therefore makes suggestions for the design of promotional material which basically relates to the handling of arguments of environmental protection in terms of legislation and consumer protection.[129] Besides these national initiatives the *International Chamber of Commerce* (*ICC*) is placed which outlines specific guidelines. Therein it claims self-discipline and the consideration of the following basic principle:

"All environmental advertising should be legal, decent, honest and truthful. It should be consistent with environmental regulations and mandatory programmes and should conform to the principles of fair competition, as generally accepted in business. No advertisements or claims should be such as to impair public confidence in the efforts made by the business community to improve its ecological performance."[130]

On the same level the *European Advertising Standards Alliance* (*EASA*) exists which deals with cross-border complaints. Thereby it presents an instrument for public to point out at misleading advertisements. For example a complaint concerning a press advertisement promoting pesticides from a Belgian environmental group is forwarded

---

[127] Cp. *Longhurst, Mike*, Advertising and Sustainability: a new paradigm, in: Admap, July/August 2003, p.44
[128] Cp. *Balderjahn, Ingo*, Nachhaltiges Marketing-Management, Lucius&Lucius Verlagsgesellschaft mbH, Stuttgart, 2004, p. 189
[129] Cp. Ibid., p. 189 et seq.
[130] Cp. *International Chamber of Commerce* (Ed.), available online
http://www.iccwbo.org/home/statements_rules/rules/1996/envicod.asp (15.2.2007)

to the *Belgian self-regulating agency* (*JEP*). The advertisement, which had appeared in various French magazines, explained the importance of pesticides for the quality of fruit and vegetables, and suggested that there was no risk in their use. The complainants maintained that some pesticides currently in use might not be entirely harmless, and referred to scientific evidence and recent legislation limiting the use of pesticides. *JEP* transferred the case to the *French self-regulating agency* (*BVP*) under the cross-border procedure.[131]

It remains questioned if a self-regulating framework and an informal applied code of practice cover the need of consumers' protection nowadays. Misleading advertising messages of environmental acceptability will probably exist in future. Consumers can only protect themselves by gathering information about products. Manufacturers can only protect themselves by looking for support of the affected company.

Advertising messages in relation to environment were in the past objective and informative. However in recent years environmental oriented advertising messages show an increasing emotional tonality.[132] Thereby the message should give a convincible, authentic and trustworthy impression. It can be transmitted in relation to product, to business or to the association. Hereby *Meffert* comprises characteristics of ecological print advertising to a typology of advertisements, which is visualised in figure 7-1.

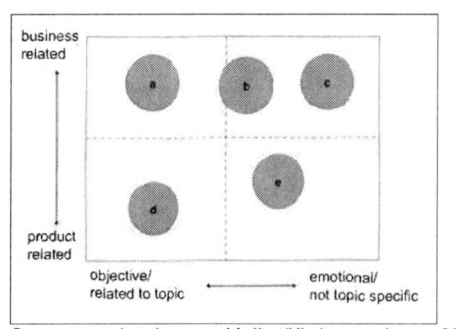

Figure 7-1: Typology of advertising in print media

Source: translated acc. to *Meffert/Kirchgeorg*, l.c., p. 321

---

[131] Cp. *European Advertising Agency* (Ed.), available online http://www.easa-alliance.org (19.02.2007)
[132] Cp. *Englfried, Justus*, Nachhaltiges Umweltmanagement, Oldenbourg Wissenschaftsverlag GmbH, München, 2004, p.164

The following examples clarify the tonality of the messages. For lack of space the ads are not portrayed completely, but are reproduced in form of a short picture description with the corresponding headlines:[133]

a) Example of a **rational targeted advertising**
    "does our waste dissolves into air? In fact: McDonald's initiates and encourages a number of seminal recycling projects" (*McDonald's*)

b) Example of a **mixed emotional/rational advertising**
    Illustration of a Buddha with Asian children in the background featuring the headline: "Environmental protection is no question of the location, but a question of the viewpoint. BASF guidelines are valid worldwide" (*BASF*)

c) Example of a **emotional targeted advertising**
    Illustration of a comic stork who claims "acting jointly..." to which the frog replies "for the sake of the environment" (*The Group of Tengelmann*)

d) Example of a **predominant rational targeted product advertising**
    Illustration of a bunch of bananas from worm's-eye view in centre combined with a descriptive statement at the right. On top the slogan "The only thing what affects our organic bananas is the sunlight" (Porridge from *Hipp*)

e) Example of a **emotional targeted product advertising**
    Illustration of a forest with a dishwasher and deer in foreground, featuring the headline "Psssst. Our most quiet dishwasher is now also the most economical." (Öko-Favorit 8081 of *AEG*)

Emotional targeted product- and business advertising activates consumers to think about its environmental respectively social pattern. Moreover consumers should be motivated to change their actual purchasing decisions.

Good examples for the educational function in regard to society are federal run 'drink-driving campaigns' and 'do not smoke campaigns'. However there are pioneers which are aware of their influence of society. Thus *Benetton* showed a mix of black

---

[133] Cp. *Meffert, Heribert*, Marketing: Grundlagen der Absatzpolitik, Gabler-Verlag, Wiesbaden, 7. rev. Ed, 1993, I.c., p. 322 et seqq.

and white people. Here advertising helped to implement awareness of new social dimensions by portrayal of multiracial situations. Another current example is *Procter & Gamble* with the advertising for their brand *Dove* in which a variety of women are portrayed who do not correspond to the ideal female body.

Both examples indicate that new unusual ideas and innovations in advertising can pay off positively for a business' image improvement. A combination of sustainable and lifestyle advertising is moreover needed to reach the consumer which feel sated with ecological messages.

7.2.2 Public Relations

The rising intensity of public criticism e.g. by the *Clean Cloth Campaign* results in a rising importance of the relationship between business and stakeholders. Business cannot afford to possess a negative image in a market with hard competition. Facing this background business are challenged in their ability to communicate. Thereby sustainable related public relations is close to the sustainable oriented corporate policy, culture and to the applied strategies of a business. A business can lose its trustworthiness in public through contradicting and inconsistent expressions of opinions by its employees. Target groups of a sustainable related PR activity are besides employees and general public also experts, associations and initiatives.

Different means exist to mirror the approach for a sustainable information policy; the following measures exist:

- Press conferences, press publications
- Sustainable reports, business reports
- Appearance on intra- and internet
- Codes of Conduct
- Company journals, anniversary issues
- Plant visits (e.g. open days)
- Charitable trusts
- Sponsoring of scientific projects in regard to environmental and social protection
- Eco sponsoring
- Consumer hotlines
- Association work
- Environmental and social oriented employee training

- Ideas and innovation competitions
- Exchange with neighbourhood
- Initiatives for sustainable management (e.g. Global Compact).

Possibilities for a proactive influence of public opinion are not limited to traditional fields of PR. Customer groups with low level of information can be reached for example by participating in or supporting of scientific symposia, co-operation with NGOs or organising trainee seminars for journalists as well as by targeted co-operation with schools or universities.[134] These examples mirror some instruments of the dialogue which is understood as communication between two or more persons for reciprocal understanding, problem- and conflict resolution. It is an interactive, bilateral and argumentative way of communication.[135]

An example for an intensive dialogue with stakeholders is the multinational company *Procter & Gamble*. In the beginning of the 1980ies public criticised enormously water pollutants deriving from washing powder. *WAGE* was the first dialogue programme initiated by top management to discuss washing and water pollution control. Meanwhile *Procter & Gamble* applies this instrument not for conflict resolution but as a tool for proactive conflict avoidance. In co-operation with scientists of *Procter & Gamble* and other attendants a discussion pool whereby the resulting information is published to educate interested professional categories or lay-public. Thus the '*Falkensteiner Gespräche*' serve for educating consumers in terms of product safety towards skin and possible allergies; whereas *HAGE* serves for an exchange of views in the field of cosmetics, hair and health.[136]

A discourse offers the chance for promoting sustainable aspects of products as well as for communicating a serious acceptance of social and environmental responsibility. Moreover conversations and discussions detect the target groups' motives and their prospective behaviour. Communicating on sustainable issues is thus a vehicle to settle or improve a brand image, to install reputation or to participate actively in public debate. However if sustainability is only used as a communicational

---

[134] Cp. *Wüstenhagen, Rolf, Villiger, Alex, Meyer, Arnt,* Jenseits der Öko-Nische, Birkhäuser Verlag AG, Basel, 2000, p. 282 et seq.
[135] Cp. *Balderjahn, Ingo,* Nachhaltiges Marketing-Management, Lucius&Lucius Verlagsgesellschaft mbH, Stuttgart, 2004, p. 131
[136] Cp. *Procter & Gamble Service GmbH*, Im Dialog, Available online http://www.procterundgamble.de/dialog/index.shtml (19.02.2007)

tool the danger exists that it may develop into a PR Gag. Mistrust may occur if measures, actions and programmes of a business do not suit the communicated content. Actions should not follow the maxim 'walk the talk' but should 'talk the walk'.[137]

7.2.3 Labelling

A variety of ecological labels, standards and trademarks exists on the market. Most consumers are not able to recognize which individual and ecological additional values arise from the purchase of the corresponding product category. Instead of creating transparency the 'label salad' confuses consumers and provokes mistrust, in many cases.[138]

Sustainable- respectively eco-labels are used for marking products and services which are more environmental- and social acceptable than comparable offers of the same product group. While labels can be used by business as sustainable profiling, they serve as practical orientation- and decision support for retail and consumers.[139] Basically one can distinguish between three kinds of labels:

- legislative labelling (e.g. symbols for Ordinance on Hazardous Substances),
- volunteer quality- and sustainable labels, certified according to criteria of independent accreditation agencies (e.g. Blauer Engel),
- business- respectively association specific eco labels (e.g. 'Purewear' at Otto).[140]

Many labels suggest the impression of marking a product which fulfils specific ecological or social aspects throughout the whole life from production till disposal. Analysis and comparisons are necessary for business to apply a trustworthy label. Comparing the labels *PEFC* and *FSC* which compete in the timber industry the following basic differences can be named:

- No transparency of *PEFC*: summary reports are only available for *FSC*.

---

[137] Cp. *Hardtke, Arnd; Prehn, Marco* (Ed.), Perspektiven der Nachhaltigkeit, Vom Leitbild zur Erfolgsstrategie, Betriebswirtschaftlicher Verlag Dr. Th. Gabler GmbH, Wiesbaden, 2001, p. 222
[138] Cp. *Wüstenhagen, Rolf, Villiger, Alex, Meyer, Arnt,* Jenseits der Öko-Nische, Birkhäuser Verlag AG, Basel, 2000, p. 129 et seq.
[139] Cp. *Balderjahn, Ingo,* Nachhaltiges Marketing-Management, Lucius&Lucius Verlagsgesellschaft mbH, Stuttgart, 2004, p. 190
[140] Cp. Ibid., p. 190

- Conflict of interests: governments and wood industry have been involved in establishing *PEFC* whereas independent non-governmental organisations established standard for *FSC*.
- Social issues are not regarded by at *PEFC* but at *FSC*.

Similar difficulties can be found in all industries. Eco-tex the first label approach in the textile and clothing industry suggests consumers to purchase a 'harmless, environmental friendly and trustful' garment. The subsequent disadvantages can be detected in comparison with the 'European Marguerite':

- Eco-tex standards could be fulfilled by 90% of all textile products, eco-flower standards are set so that 30% of each industry (the best-available) could be certified.
- Eco-tex refers only to the product and not to production, eco flower regards the ecological impact of the manufacturing product.
- Eco-tex claims to send one sample for certification, eco flower demands a sample from each product, meaning e.g. spinning mills send a sample of each yarn for certification.

The *eco flower* extends to the manufacturing inquiry e.g. air and water emissions. In order to involve production ecology *eco-tex* initiated the standard 100plus. It is based on standard 100 which relates to the product and standard 1000 which checks the ecological impact of the production site. Because the *eco-flower* and *eco-tex* lack of the social aspects (e.g. fair working conditions, child work, etc) textile and clothing companies need to refer to specific social labels, such as *SA 8000* to communicate sustainability by a label.[141]

Thus a sustainable label which refers to all parts of a products' life cycle could be an important tool for consumer information. In this regard *TÜV Rhineland* drew up the label '*ecoproof*'. The basic idea is to brand textiles, which are produced environmentally sound (based on certification of *EMAS*), socially fair (standards according to *ILO*) and are tested against possible harmful substances. For giving an informative picture of the product a pass is attached which publishes the textile origin and history. This idea was enforced by *Steilmann* and their implementation of a product profile in the 1990ies. However in spring 2007 *Timberland* picks up this idea in line with the campaign 'Which footprint do you want to leave?' and introduces a so called 'nutritional label'. The index names the manufacturing facility, the social and

---

[141] See Appendix for detail description

environmental impact. For the latter it reveals e.g. the raw material, the amount of chemicals and the used energy in production.[142]

Approaches for a global textile and clothing label are still in their infancies as well as the idea for a sustainable label. An international label may be realized in co-operation with an association or initiative such as the *Global Compact*. Herein the *Global Organic Textile Standard* could pose with its target formulated in the following wording: "to define world-wide recognised requirements that ensure organic status of textiles, from harvesting of the raw materials, through environmentally and socially responsible manufacturing up to labelling in order to provide a credible assurance to the end consumer."[143]

It remains to be adhered that the amount of labels should be kept relatively low in order to provoke less confusion as well as to popularise and widespread one unique standard. By promoting one already existing label permanently or by creating a more credible label concept, the efficiency and credibility of a label can be increased. Influencing parameters thereby relate to the reputation and credibility of the certifying agency and its control scheme as well as to the demands and transparency of the certification requirements. Consequently there is a lot to do in the area of informative product labels to help consumers learn what is sustainable and what is not.

7.2.4 Sponsoring

Sponsoring became popular from the area of sports. Since the 1980ies sponsoring budgets have reached immense amounts. Sports sponsoring provides business a clear image of 'young and dynamic' or 'active and successful'. Instead of an image transfer eco- respectively societal marketing symbolizes the acceptance of ecological and societal responsibility as well as its communication.[144] Sustainable sponsoring as part of the communication policy allows a business by provision of physical and financial resources to use sponsored social or ecological projects or to make use of

---

[142] Cp. *Dowideit, Anette*, Hauptquartier in der Blockhütte, in: DIE WELT, 19.12.2006
[143] Cp. *International Association Natural Textile Industry e.V.* (Ed.), Available online http://www.global-standard.org (19.02.2007)
[144] Cp. *Belz, Christian* (Ed.), Akzente im innovativen Marketing, Verlag THEXIS [Forschungsinstituts für Absatz und Handel an der Universität], St. Gallen, 1998, p. 222

organisations or individuals which work in a social or ecological area for its own communication purpose.[145]

For determination of the sponsoring goals the target group needs to be identified at first. Strategy and measures have to be planned exactly, so that the sponsoring activity can be integrated into the existing marketing- and communication concept of a business. For single measures concretised sponsorships need to be chosen, performances and contracts need to be designed appropriately. In regard to the sponsoring strategy measures for determination of the sponsored area, kind and content need to be taken between sponsor and sponsored. Matches of the contents can arise in reference to responsibility, region, product, image, target group and know-how.[146]

Sponsoring can be found in all industries and for many support areas as the following examples illustrate:

- *Marks & Spencer* is member of the business community '*One Per Cent – club*', committed to investing at least 1% of pre-tax profits into community improvement programmes,[147]
- *Nike* participates in WWF Climate Savers programme focussing on the reduction of greenhouse gas emissions like carbondioxide,[148]
- *BMW* engages in South Africa for HIV/ AIDS prevention,[149]
- *Henkel* supports non-profit projects organised by its employees on a voluntary basis by physical or financial resources,[150]
- *HypoVereinsbank* engages in the research group for the local *Agenda 21*, an institution to support local sustainable activities by financial service providers,[151]
- *METRO* Group is the main financial sponsor of the federal association *Deutsche Tafel e. V.* and supports poor people in Germany with nutrients.[152]

---

[145] Cp. *Balderjahn, Ingo, Nachhaltiges Marketing-Management*, Lucius&Lucius Verlagsgesellschaft mbH, Stuttgart, *2004*, p. 193
[146] Cp. *Engelfried, Justus*, Nachhaltiges Umweltmanagement, Oldenbourg Wissenschaftsverlag GmbH, München, 2004, p. 165
[147] Cp. *Marks & Spencer Group plc.* (Ed.),Corporate Social Responsibility Report 2006, Warrington, 2006, p. 26
[148] Cp. *Nike Inc.* (Ed.), Corporate Responsibility Report 2005, Beaverton, 2005, p.60
[149] Cp. *Bayrische Motorenwerke AG* (Ed.), Sustainable Value Report BMW Group 2006, München, 2005, p.82
[150] Cp. *Henkel KGaA* (Ed.), Nachhaltigkeitsbericht 2005, Düsseldorf, 2006, p. 26
[151] Cp. *Bayerische Hypo- und Vereinsbank AG* (Ed.), Nachhaltigkeitsbericht 2005, München, 2005, p. 45

A new and innovative kind of sponsoring is the determination of profit- or turnover quota in favour of projects. Thereby as inherent part of the corporate philosophy the sales volume of products and services is directly linked to sustainable measures.[153] One often speaks of 'Corporate Giving'.

The German brewery *Krombacher* protects one square meter tropical rain forest for each sold beer crate. Parallel *Krombacher* invites their online customer to donor 1.50€ and in return plants a tree to equalize emitted pollutants. *IKEA* co-operates with *UNICEF* to finance projects for compulsory education by donating 1€ of each sold soft toy.[154] *Otto* forwards 10€ of each sold jeans from the brand 'Youth against labels' to the *Foundation for Sustainable Agriculture and Forestry*, which supports the project '*Cotton made in Africa*' and therewith African peasants.[155]

Ecological and social engagement gains a positive feedback and helps to improve the image from the employees as well as from the outside point of view. But by running an untrustworthy campaign the danger of harming the business' image as well as losing the trust of consumers in such campaigns arises. Precondition for success of this instrument is thus "the agreement between the sponsored individuals respectively projects and the represented authentic targets of a business."[156]

7.3 Price policy

Possible measures concerning price policy are not as multifaceted as the marketing decisions in communication – or product political authority of a business. Price policy aims at defining and comparing alternative price demands towards potential customers. Moreover the price policy decides for an alternative and for its implementation while utilizing the decision-making leeway which is limited by company internal and external factors.[157]

---

[152] Cp. *Metro AG* (Ed.), Nachhaltigkeitsbericht 2006, Verantwortlich handeln – Zukunft gestalten, Düsseldorf, 2006, p. 32
[153] Cp. *Engelfried, Justus*, Nachhaltiges Umweltmanagement, Oldenbourg Wissenschaftsverlag GmbH, München, 2004, p.165
[154] Cp. *Ikea Deutschland GmbH & Co. KG* (Ed.), Social & Environmental Responsibility Report 2005, p. 45
[155] Cp. *Otto (GmbH & Co KG)* (Ed.), Unternehmerische Verantwortung bei OTTO, Hamburg, 2007, p.9
[156] Cp. *Balderjahn, Ingo*, Nachhaltiges Marketing-Management, Lucius&Lucius Verlagsgesellschaft mbH, Stuttgart, 2004, p. 193
[157] Cp. *Meffert, Heribert*, Marketing: Grundlagen der Absatzpolitik, Gabler-Verlag, Wiesbaden, 7. rev. Ed, 1993, l.c., p. 262

Instruments of marketing

According to *Kotler* price political decisions are made by the following:

1. "primary determination of price, which is necessary for new products, entry of new markets and tendering for a unique contract,
2. change of price, initiated by company due to demand- and price changes as well as special offers for demand support,
3. change of price initiated by competitors and
4. determination of the ideal price relationship of products from one product line, which are connected by price and /or costs."[158]

As well as for conventional products the price finding for sustainable products can be made costs-, demand- or competitor oriented. Thereby prices are basically justified by higher production costs due to the implementation of ecological raw material or social fair production processes.[159] Moreover a low volume of sales combined with a low number of units add on the production costs. These costs are passed on to the customers. Business at the same time can profit from the higher price range of sustainable products. However the actual willingness to pay more for socio-ecological products is even divergent for environmental accessible consumers.[160] Sustainable products need to be characterised with certain product safety and - quality measures to reach the customer, as e.g. in the area of food in which organic products are connected with healthiness. For expensive sustainable products the most important purchase argument is the perceived higher social value of a product, e.g. 'ethical fashion brands' communicate prestige and luxury.

Several price calculations are applicable for sustainable oriented products. Among others the method of mixed calculation is often used. Herein prices of conventional and sustainable products of one market segment are equated, which enables that the customer can decide for "his better performing" product without any price pressure.[161]

---

[158] Cp. *Kotler, Philip, Bliemel, Friedhelm*, Marketing-Management, Schäffer-Poeschel Verlag, Stuttgart, 8. rev. Ed, p.262
[159] Cp. *Wüstenhagen, Rolf, Villiger, Alex, Meyer, Arnt,* Jenseits der Öko-Nische, Birkhäuser Verlag AG, Basel, 2000, p. 43
[160] Cp. *Baldjahn, Ingo*, Nachhaltiges Marketing-Management, Lucius&Lucius Verlagsgesellschaft mbH, Stuttgart, 2004, p.186
[161] Cp. *Meffert, Heribert, Meffert, Heribert*, Marketing: Grundlagen der Absatzpolitik, Gabler-Verlag, Wiesbaden, 7. rev. Ed, 1993, l.c., p. 244

The global discounter *Walmart* offered organic cotton tops sold for less than $10, pants for less than $14 in the USA in 2006.[162] The Suisse retail chain *Coop* offers organic cotton clothing under the product line *Naturaline* without price surcharge.
In Germany the purchase of eco fashion without price premium was until not possible. The biggest dispatcher of eco wear *Hess Natur* offers its goods still for higher prices. *Otto* launched in 2003 its organic cotton line '*Purewear*', with an average surcharge of ca. 30%.[163] However since spring 2007 the introduction of an organic cotton line at *H&M* enables as well German consumers to purchase eco wear without price pressure.[164]

Price differentiations which work in another way are possible: time oriented price differentiations can be applied if one aims at a short-time competitive advantage. Herein one can choose between the skimming- or penetration pricing strategy. High introduction prices of a new sustainable product aim at absorption of the buying power. Penetration pricing enables a fast market penetration with e.g. low prices. This can result in a fast growing market share and thus a realizable economies of scale.[165] Both pricing strategies can come into conflict with other targets of a business and thus have to be applied carefully.

Next to the method of time oriented pricing a differentiation in regard to customer segments can be applied. Therein different prices are set for each customer group according to sustainable orientation. High prices are set for areas in which sustainable acting consumers are prepared to pay for it. Price differentiations of this kind are mostly applied in enterprises, which launch products in a variety of countries with different characteristics.[166]

For a marketing beyond the niche it remains open to prove if products can be offered at the same or at a lower price as conventional products. Or if it is more promising to

---

[162] *Gunther, Marc*, Organic for everyone: the Wal-Mart way, in: Fortune Magazine, 31.07.2006
[163] Cp. *Brodde, Kirsten*, Ottos neue Kleider, in: Greenpeace Magazine, 2004, Magazine No. 3, p. 56
[164] Cp. Press release: New H&M collection features organic cotton, 19.02.2007, available online: http://www.hm.com/de/presse___press.nhtml
[165] Cp. *Wüstenhagen, Rolf, Villiger, Alex, Meyer, Arnt*, Jenseits der Öko-Nische, Birkhäuser Verlag AG, Basel, 2000, p.48
[166] Cp. *Meffert, Heribert*, Marketing: Grundlagen der Absatzpolitik, Gabler-Verlag, Wiesbaden, 7. rev. Ed, 1993, l.c., p. 244

keep a (remote) additional charge due to the function of the price as quality signal.[167] Besides financial undertakings there are as well measures to enforce sustainable products which comprise incentives for returning old products or competitive leasing contracts.

7.4 Distribution

The term distribution covers all decisions and actions, which are in connection with the product on its way to the end-consumer. On the one hand ecological oriented distribution deals with the development of old and the building of new distribution channels in terms of product sales and disposal of products and its packaging. On the other hand logistic systems focus on conserving resources. Logistic systems aim at transferring products at the requested time in the right amount to the required place in unchanged quality.[168] An organisation can optimise distribution by choice of distribution channels in regard to sustainable criteria and in particular by the implementation of sustainable standards throughout the channel and throughout the physical distribution.[169]

Hereby regulations on packaging (concept of the dual waste management) and on close-loop waste management set the general framework for redistribution and therewith influence the development of closed cycles of matter, which can only be realized in co-operation with retail.[170] Thus in regard to legislative changes in May 2006 retail and bottling industry introduced the *German Deposit System GmbH (DPG)*. Thereby retail is obliged to redeem all beverages and to refund the deposit of all kinds of beverage packaging they put in circulation. Just small shops with less than 200 m³ may limit the withdrawal to the brands they sell. In line with the *DPG*-system cans and single-use bottles have to be marked with a new label. Furthermore an electronic readable barcode and an additional security identifier should be printed on.[171]

---

[167] Cp. *Wüstenhagen, Rolf, Villiger, Alex, Meyer, Arnt,* Jenseits der Öko-Nische, Birkhäuser Verlag AG, Basel, 2000, p. 48
[168] Cp. *Meffert, Heribert; Kirchgeorg, Manfred,* Marktorientiertes Umweltmanagement, Schäffer Poeschel Verlag, Stuttgart, 3. rev. Ed., 1998, p. 345
[169] Cp. *Balderjahn, Ingo,* Nachhaltiges Marketing-Management, Lucius&Lucius Verlagsgesellschaft mbH, Stuttgart, 2004, p. 194
[170] Cp. Ibid., p. 194
[171] Cp. *Deutsche Pfandsystem Gmbh* (Ed.), available online http://dpg-pfandsystem.de/servlet/PB/menu/-1/index.html (19.02.2007)

The example of the Suisse wholesaler *Bataillard* demonstrates the possibilities of co-operation between wine merchants and suppliers. In line with the *top50-system* *Bataillard* initiated a system to reuse whine bottles in the early 1990ies. Therefore they basically changed the volume of bottles to 0.5lt and to screw caps. Distribution of the whine to Switzerland is carried out in cisterns instead of bottles whereas distribution inside Switzerland is carried out in crates of 15 bottles. Besides ecological advantages this system supports as well the Suisse bottling industry by forming a barrier to market entry. Meanwhile the system established throughout Switzerland, and is accepted by bottlers, catering, retail and consumers.

Besides the co-operation of manufacturers and retail in areas of redistribution further sustainable oriented possibilities arise. Therefore I would like to point at the acquisitioning area of distribution policy (in which the establishing of a connection to market participants is focussed).
On the one hand separate distribution channels can be established e.g. an ecological oriented retail business as subsidiary (e.g. *Aldi* and its American subsidiary *Trader Joe's*; *Unilever* acquired *Ben&Jerry*) or a franchisee of an established business (*The Body Shop*). On the other hand ecological products can be integrated into the conventional sales programme, this may lead to a reorganisation of the whole range of goods.[172] Hereunto a successful example can be given by the organic food industry. The distribution changed from direct sales on farms in 1980ies and wholefood shops in the 1990ies. In the last years the integration of organic food into the sales programme of discounters lead to enormous market penetration (e.g. Suisse retailer *Coop* and its product line *Naturaplan*, German distributor *Rewe* and its product line *Füllhorn*). Thereby consumers beyond the niche are motivated and the introduced organic food corners enables to target consumers directly.[173]

In line retail needs to inform customers at the point of purchase. Herein manufacturers and retail should collaborate by common concepts for merchandising or sales promotion. Nevertheless relationships between manufacturers and retail provide a high potential of conflict due to different sustainable oriented strategies, as figure 7-2 visualises.

---

[172] Cp. *Wüstenhagen, Rolf, Villiger, Alex, Meyer, Arnt,* Jenseits der Öko-Nische, Birkhäuser Verlag AG, Basel, 2000, p. 49
[173] Cp. *Wüstenhagen, Rolf, Villiger, Alex, Meyer, Arnt,* Jenseits der Öko-Nische, Birkhäuser Verlag AG, Basel, 2000, p. 116

Instruments of marketing   Page 77

Figure 7-2: Conflict potentials between retail and manufacturers

	MANUFACTURER		
	defensive	selective	proactive
RETAIL defensive	ignorance		complete environment
RETAIL selective		cooperation	selective environment
RETAIL proactive	complete substitution	selective substitution	innovative cooperation

Source: translated acc. to. *Meffert/Kirchgeorg*, p. 353

The logistical system is of further importance for sustainable designed distribution. The focus is basically on resources (raw material, energy) or on environmental related facts (emissions, waste). Ecological criteria which help for evaluation of alternative transport possibilities are according to *Balderjahn:* environmental friendliness, safety and effective utilisation of transportation means as well as reduction and optimisation of the required flow of traffic. By introduction of distribution centres next to urban areas results in a sustainable optimisation of commodity flows by bundling. Empty runs and multiple runs are prevented to a large extent so that less runs are necessary).[174]

Such concepts are for example offered by the logistical provider *Fiege*, which plans and implements the logistics for industry and retail businesses. *Fiege* group managed to unite economical and ecological dimensions, among others the following performances characterise the concept of the group:

- Intelligent clustering of transport to reduce the total necessary traffic,
- Change from trucks to transportation by train and ship,

---
[174] Cp. *Balderjahn, Ingo,* Nachhaltiges Marketing-Management, Lucius&Lucius Verlagsgesellschaft mbH, Stuttgart, 2004, p. 194

- 50% of the warehouse areas are not asphaltiert, but gepflastert and contain biotopes to lead surface water to groundwater,
- Usage of environmental acceptable building materials,
- Usage of renewable resources,
- Reusable package system to motivate retail and manufacturers to abandon conventional packaging materials respectively appropriate recycling for not reusable material from manufacturers abroad,
- Dialogue with manufacturers and retail to develop packaging alternatives.[175]

Placement policy is challenged by the extension of the distribution channels for sustainable products. Successful examples for placement possibilities can be given by the organic food industry. Its distribution policy indicates that a marketing beyond the niche explores unconventional distribution channels. Manufacturers, retail, press, consumers, NGOs and logistic companies thereby can help to offer sustainable products area-wide.

8 Conclusion and outlook

Sustainability-marketing moves within the area of conflict: between socio-ecological problems on the other hand and the satisfaction of customer needs on the other hand. It is certain that sustainable products need to penetrate in the long-term to conform the approach of sustainable development. However sustainable oriented marketing must not solely focus on a marketing oriented promotion of sustainable products and services, because sustainable development can only be achieved by means of sustainable consumption. A marketing for sustainability is thus needed, which provokes a change of customers' awareness towards an increased sustainable oriented behaviour. Therefore objective and educational advertising campaigns are required. In the future besides enterprises and policy it will be consumer associations, environmental initiatives as well as charitable trusts which need to initiate a professional communication policy to arbitrate between public interest and the individual consumer. Thereby the focus must be on introducing and establishing new arguments and values.

---

[175] Cp. *Meffert, Heribert; Kirchgeorg, Manfred*, Marktorientiertes Umweltmanagement, Schäffer Poeschel Verlag, Stuttgart, 3. rev. Ed., 1998, INSERT 34

This study presents the progressing development from eco-marketing to sustainability-marketing and mirrors the previous position of the debate. At this place it should be noted, that scientific research is still in its infancy and one can only revert to a few examples from experience. Finally a demand exists for further research. Thus the different implementation possibilities of the concept 'sustainable development' on the strategic level offer an exiting research area. Here ecology is attributed more importance than social aspects. This weighing may change in the course of time, because the reputation of an ecological and social responsible business can only be build up and maintained in long-term if indeed a superior assumption of responsibility exists.

Business are as well challenged in the face of entrepreneurial sustainable marketing on the operative level. Besides a top quality of products sustainable purchase consumption requires an ecological and social acceptable production and disposal process. This demands a certain trust from customer to its 'supplier'. Tasks such as the stabilisation of the ecosystem or the commitment to social justice add to the marketing instruments. Product political measures such as life cycle analyses and appropriate package solutions are needed for a sustainable performance of the enterprise. Likewise distribution and price policy contribute to success. To come over the dictate of price sustainable marketing needs to aim on motive alliances, on clever flanking of socio-ecological aspects and conventional purchase criteria as well as on an emotional communication policy. It could be interesting to analyse which kind of communication – ultra emotional or objective rational – succeeds in meeting the various target groups or if a combination is more promising. For meeting broader target groups communication tools in line with an open dialogue, sponsoring or volunteering are possible. 'Ecotainment' is hereunto an emerging idea and needs to be watched.

However it remains important that enterprises, policy and consumers recognize the indispensability of responsible acting for a positive environmental and social future. To annotate in terms of Voltaire: "We are not only responsible for what we do, but we are as well responsible what we don't do."

List of literature

1. Books

Balderjahn, Ingo, Nachhaltiges Marketing-Management, Lucius&Lucius Verlagsgesellschaft mbH, Stuttgart, 2004, ISBN 3-8282-0188-1.

Belz, Christian (Ed.), Akzente im innovativen Marketing, Verlag THEXIS [Forschungsinstituts für Absatz und Handel an der Universität], St. Gallen, 1998, ISBN 3-908545-34-X.

Belz, Frank-Martin, Integratives Öko-Marketing. Erfolgreiche Vermarktung ökologischer Produkte und Leistungen, Deutscher Universitäts-Verlag GmbH, Betriesbswirtschaftlicher Verlag Dr. Th. Gabler GmbH, 1. Ed., Wiesbaden, 2001. ISBN 3-8244-9047-1.

Engelfried, Justus, Nachhaltiges Umweltmanagement, Oldenbourg Wissenschaftsverlag GmbH, München, 2004, ISBN 3-4862-0012-7.

Fischer, Guido, Ökologie und Management, Eine Einführung für Praxis und Studium, Versus Verlag, 1. Ed., Zürich, 1996, ISBN 3-9081-4335-2

Grettenberger, Dunja, Umweltschutz und Umweltbewusstsein, Ansatzpunkte einer effizienten Umweltpolitik, Verlag Wissenschaft und Praxis, Berlin, 1996

Hardtke, Arnd; Prehn, Marco (Ed.), Perspektiven der Nachhaltigkeit, Vom Leitbild zur Erfolgsstrategie, Betriebswirtschaftlicher Verlag Dr. Th. Gabler GmbH, Wiesbaden, 2001, ISBN 3-4091-1715-6.

Kotler, Philip; Armstrong, Gary; Saunders, John; Wong, Veronica, Principles of Marketing, Prentice Hall Inc, Second European Edition, New Jersey/ USA, 1999.

Kotler, Philip, Bliemel, Friedhelm, Marketing-Management, Schäffer-Poeschel Verlag, Stuttgart, 8. rev. Ed, 1995, ISBN 3-7910-0882-X

Linne, Gudrun, Schwarz, Michael (ed.), Handbuch Nachhaltige Entwicklung: Wie ist nachhaltiges Wirtschaften machbar?, Verlag Leske + Budrich, Opladen, 2003. ISBN 3-8100-3758-3.

Meffert, Heribert, Marketing: Grundlagen der Absatzpolitik, Gabler-Verlag, Wiesbaden, 7. rev. Ed, 1993, ISBN 3-4096-9015-X

Meffert, Heribert; Kirchgeorg, Manfred, Marktorientiertes Umweltmanagement, Schäffer Poeschel Verlag, Stuttgart, 3. rev. Ed., 1998, ISBN 3-7910-1147-2.

Röttger, Ulrike, PR Kampagnen: Über die Inszenierung von Öffentlichkeit, VS Verlag für Sozialwissenschaften, Wiesbaden, 3. rev. Ed., 2006, ISBN 3-5314-2950-7.

Türck, Rainer, Das ökologische Produkt, Verlag Wissenschaft & Praxis, Ludwigsburg/Berlin, 2. Ed., 1991, ISBN 3-9282-3809-4.

Weber, Christoph, Scherhorn, Gerhard (Ed.), Nachhaltiger Konsum – Auf dem Weg zur gesellschaftlichen Verankerung, oekom Verag, München, 2003, ISBN 3-9882-4485-X

Wüstenhagen, Rolf, Villiger, Alex, Meyer, Arnt, Jenseits der Öko-Nische, Birkhäuser Verlag AG, Basel, 2000, ISBN 3-7643-6247-2.

Ulrich, Hans, Systemorientiertes Management: das Werk von Hans Ulrich, Haupt Verlag, Bern/Stuttgart/Wien, 2001, ISBN 3-2580-6359-1.

Zadek, Simon, The Civil Corporation: The New Economy of Corporate Citizenship, Earthscan Publications, London, 2001, p. 105 et seq., ISBN 1-8538-3997-3.

Zimmermann, Rolf, New Business Style, Gellius Verlag GmbH, Herrsching am Ammersee, 2005, ISBN 3-9361-7914-X.

2. Journal articles

Brodde, Kirsten, Ottos neue Kleider, in: Greenpeace Magazine, 2004, Magazine 3, p. 56

Bunk, Burkhardt, Corporate Citizenship und Marketing: Wie Synergien erschlossen werden, in: Absatzwirtschaft, 2003, Magazine No. 10, p. 26 et seq.

Burger, Katrin, Politik mit der Einkaufstüte, in: die Tageszeitung, Berlin, Bonn, 02.04.2003

Dowideit, Anette, Hauptquartier in der Blockhütte, in: DIE WELT, 19.12.2006

FINANZtest Magazin (Ed.), Grüne Gewinne, in: FINANZtest, 2006, Magazine No. 6, p.39 et seq.

FINANZtest Magazin (Ed.), Grüne Geldanlage: Die Guten, in: FINANZtest, 2007, Magazine No. 2, p. 24 et seqq.

Geldmancher, Frauke in: Grünes Bewusstsein – Chance oder Marketinggag? in: X-Ray/global style and fashion, 2006, Magazine No. 4, p. 24

Gunther, Marc, Organic for everyone: the Wal-Mart way, in: Fortune Magazine, 31.07.2006

Hahn, Tobias, Scheermesser, Mandy, Das Nachhaltigkeitsengagement deutscher Unternehmen, in: UmweltWirtschaftsForum, 2005, Magazine No. 2, p. 70-75

Hoffritz, Jutta: Eine Pille gegen Einsamkeit, in: DIE ZEIT, 28.09.2006, Nr. 40.

Longhurst, Mike, Advertising and Sustainability: a new paradigm, in: Admap, July/August 2003, p. 44

Kichgeorg, Manfred, Nachhaltigkeits- Marketing, in: UmweltWirtschaftsForum, 2002; Magazine No. 4, p. 4-11

Margolis, Joshua D. & Walsh, James P., Misery Loves Companies: Rethinking Social Initiatives by Business, In: Administrative Science Quarterly Vol. 48 (2003), p. 268-305

Maschewski, Alexandra, Moralische Mode: Schluss mit Ausreden, rein in die Ökoklamotten, in: DIE WELT, 17.02.2007

Palass, Brigitta, Chemische Reinigung, in: Manager Magazin, 1999, Magazine No. 9, p. 136

Schaltegger, Stefan, in: Nachhaltiges Wirtschaften, Handelsblatt, 12. Juni 2006

Schmidt, Frithjof in: Huber, Stephan, Fair Trade muss Standard werden, in: X-Ray/ global style and fashion, 2006, Magazine No. 4, l.c., p. 28

Stäsche, Peter, Bio - gestern und heute, in: *Markt & Medien*, 2007, Magazine No. 3, p. 1

3. Further publications

3. a Business brochures

Bank Sarasin & Cie AG (Ed.), Nachhaltigkeitsstudie „Just do it" - aber verantwortungsbewusst, Basel, 2006

Bank Sarasin & Cie AG (Ed.), Mitteilung an die Medien: Im Überblick die Nachhaltigkeit verschiedener Branchen, Basel, 2006

BASF AG (Ed.), Ökoeffizienz Analyse „made by BASF" verspricht eine mehrfache Rendite, Speech on Envitec "Von Ökoeffizienz zu nachhaltiger Entwicklung in Unternehmen", Düsseldorf, 15./16.05.01. Available online
http://corporate.basf.com/en/sustainability

Bayerische Hypo- und Vereinsbank AG (Ed.), Nachhaltigkeitsbericht 2005, München, 2005

Bayrische Motorenwerke AG (Ed.), Sustainable Value Report BMW Group 2006, München, 2005

Coop (Ed.), Regionale Produkte, available online
http://www.coop.ch/naturaplan/bio_spezialitaeten/regionale_produzenten-de.htm
(21.12.2006)

Corporate Knights Inc., Karen Kun (Ed.), Toronto, 14.01.2007, available online
www.global100.org

H & M (Ed.), Press release: New H&M collection features organic cotton, 19.02.2007, available online http://www.hm.com/de/presse_press.nhtml
Henkel KGaA (Ed.), Nachhaltigkeitsbericht 2005, Düsseldorf, 2006

Henkel KGaA (Ed.), Nachhaltigkeitsbericht 2006, Düsseldorf, 2007

Ikea Deutschland GmbH & Co. KG (Ed.), Social & Environmental Responsibility Report 2005

Lafuma Group (Ed.), Sustainable Development Report Lafuma Group 2005, Anneyron, 2005

Nike Inc. (Ed.), Corporate Responsibility Report 2005, Beaverton, 2005

Marks & Spencer Group plc. (Ed.),Corporate Social Responsibility Report 2006, Warrington, 2006

Metro AG (Ed.), Nachhaltigkeitsbericht 2006, Verantwortlich handeln – Zukunft gestalten, Düsseldorf, 2006

Otto (GmbH & Co KG) (Ed.), Brochure: Corporate Responsibility at Otto, Hamburg, 2007

Otto (GmbH & Co KG) (Ed.), Brochure: Unternehmerische Verantwortung bei OTTO, Hamburg, 2007

Procter & Gamble Service GmbH (Ed.), Im Dialog, Available online http://www.procterundgamble.de/dialog/index.shtml (19.02.2007)

Werner & Mertz GmbH (Ed.), Umwelterklärung 2006, Mainz, 2006

Wesselmann, Matthias, Einkauf von Bio-Lebensmitteln: Supermärkte haben die Nase vorn, Press Release, fischerAppelt Kommunikation GmbH, Hamburg, 2006

3. b Publications by associations, institutes and federal agencies

Bayerisches Staatsministerium für Umwelt, Gesundheit und Verbraucherschutz (Ed.), Informationen und Empfehlungen zur integrierten Produktpolitik (IPP) in Marketingkonzepten, München, 2005

BTE, Ökologie im Textileinzelhandel, Fachpublikation

Bundesministerium für Umwelt, Naturschutz und Reaktorsicherheit (Ed.), Umweltbewusstsein 2006, Berlin, 2006.

Bundesministerium für Umwelt, Naturschutz und Reaktorsicherheit (Ed.), Umweltbewusstsein 2002, Berlin, 2002

Deutsche Pfandsystem Gmbh (Ed.), available online http://dpg-pfandsystem.de/servlet/PB/menu/-1/index.html (19.02.2007)

European Advertising Standard (Ed.), available online http://www.easa-alliance.org (19.02.2007)

European Commission (Ed.), European Platform on Life Cycle Assessment, Ispra, Italy, available online http://lca.jrc.ec.europa.eu/lcainfohub/index.vm (20.02.2007)

Fraunhofer Institut für Lebensmitteltechnologie und Verpackung, Vol. 3: Produkt-Ökobilanz vakuumverpackter Röstkaffee, LCA Documents, Eco-Informa Press, Bayreuth, Ed. 1., 1998, ISBN/ISSN 3-928379-55-0

International Association Natural Textile Industry e.V. (Ed.), Available online http://www.global-standard.org (19.02.2007)

International Chamber of Commerce (Ed.), available online http://www.iccwbo.org/home/statements_rules/rules/1996/envicod.asp (15.2.2007)

Ministerium für Umwelt und Verkehr Baden-Württemberg (Ed.), Kooperative Ansätze im Rahmen einer integrierten Produktpolitik, Stuttgart, 2004, available online www.uvm.baden-wuerttemberg.de (20.02.2007)

McCann-Erickson / UNEP (Ed.), Brochure Can sustainability sell?, Paris, First Edition, 2002

Netzwerk COUP 21 (Ed.), Leitfaden: Management ökologischer Produkte, München, 2001, available online www.coup21.de (20.02.2007)

Umweltbundesamt (Ed.), Jahresbericht 2005, Dessau, 2006.

Umweltbundesamt (Ed.), Informationen für Wasch- und Reinigungsmittel 2006, available online http://www.umweltbundesamt.de/uba-info-daten/daten/wasch/trends.htm (21.01.2007)

WBCSD (Ed.), Brochure: Sustainability through the market. Seien kess to Success, 2001, available online www.wbcsd.org

UNEP (Ed.), Brochure: Talk the walk – advancing sustainable lifestyles through Marketing and Communications, Nairobi, Kenya, 2005, ISBN 92-807-2658-7.

WBCSD (Ed.), Brochure: Driving Success - Marketing and Sustainable Development, 2005, available online www.wbcsd.org

Zentralstelle für Berufsbildung im Einzelhandel e.V. (Ed.), Available online http://www.elearning.zbb.de (21.01.2007)

3. c Miscellaneous

BASF AG (Ed), Speech on Envitec "Von Ökoeffizienz zu nachhaltiger Entwicklung in Unternehmen", Düsseldorf , 15./16.05.01. available online http://corporate.basf.com/en/sustainability

Gabriel, Sigmar, Innovation für Wirtschaft und Umwelt, Leitmärkte der Zukunft ökologisch erobern, BMU-Innovationskonferenz, dbb Forum Berlin, 30.10.2006

Eberle, Ulrike, Das Nachhaltigkeitszeichen: ein Instrument zur Umsetzung einer nachhaltigen Entwicklung? In: Werkstattreihe Nr. 127, Freiburg: Öko-Institut e.V. Freiburg, 2001

Empacher, Claudia, Vortrag bei Tagung „Nachhaltiger Konsum? Auf dem Weg zur gesellschaftlichen Verankerung" 29./30.11.2001.

Mederer, Margit, Neue Ansätze für Design und Ökologie in der Möbelindustrie, ProÖko Servicegesellschaft ökologischer Einrichtungshäuser mbH, Workshop on Agritechnica, Hannover, 2001.

Müller, Edda, „Nachhaltiger Konsum: Utopie oder Geschäftsstrategie?", Rede auf dem Forum Nachhaltigkeit, Veranstalter: American Chamber of Commerce in Germany (AmCham Germany) am 12. April 2005 in Berlin

Troge, Andreas, Nachhaltiger Konsum – Illusion der Ökos?, Speech on the symposium of ‚GRÜN leben', Berlin, 9.12.2006

APPENDIX

National Labels

Blauer Engel   Blauer Engel labels environmental sound products from distinct product groups. The system was introduced in 1977 in Germany and is worldwide the most extended environmental related label on a volunteer basis but with governmental control. The environmental label aims at information and motivation as well as conviction and environmental engagement of producers and consumers. It relates to the relative environmental soundness on products in comparison to products from the same category. Examples for good adaption of the labels products of recycling paper. Meanwhile services like car washing devices or tickets can obtain the label. All certified products or services carry the label visibly for consumers.

During certification ecological problems occurring in the product life cycle are identified and given alternatives are judged. Only distinct critical steps are taken into account, thus avoiding a complete product eco balance. Various requirements for the certification of products and services are developed by an independent jury involving the Umweltbundesamt as well as the federal state in which the producers of the products is situated.

Miljömärkt   Miljömarkt was originated in 1989 by the Nordic Council of Ministers to introduce an environmental label valid all over Scandinavia. This is similar to the European Eco label: it regards the products' life cycle and measures the impact of the product on environment. Thus organisations gained the European Flower can use the Swan for promotion in Scandinavian countries.

Umweltzeichen	The Environmental Label was established in 1990 by the Austrian Department of the Environment and is close to the German environmental label. Most requirements for certification were adapted without major changes.

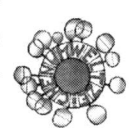

For accreditation the organisation proves the product or service itself, its production and the packaging as well as the recyclable aspect in terms of energy consumption, harmful substances and emissions. Thus the production process is given more emphasis than the German label.

Umweltzeichen stated first to forbid for wood furnishing all tropical woods due to the problem of certification of sustainable forests. Nevertheless the clause was changed to the criteria wood from sustainable foresting.

Eco label	The flower is a symbol for environmental friendly products in the EEA since 1992. The EU Eco-label drew up a set of environmental and performance criteria for judging products according to the impact on the environment. Only if products meet all criteria they can be awarded the EU Eco-label. These environmental criteria take into account all aspects of a product's life, from its production and use to its eventual disposal. This is also known as a cradle-to-grave approach. The EU Eco-label scheme can be applied generally to every kind of product or service, except food and medical goods. To name a few examples for criteria:

- limit value of toxic residues in fibres e.g. man-made cellulose: AOX < 250ppm
- limit value of air and water pollution during fibre process
- limit value of harmful substances and human health e.g. formaldehyde, heavy metals and azo dyes
- performance and durability e.g. percentage of shrinkage and colour fastness to perspiration, washing and wet rubbing, etc.

Labels for textiles and clothing

Eco-proof TÜV Rhineland brands textiles, which are produced environmentally sound, socially fair and are tested against possible harmful substances with the eco –proof label. Criteria are very strict; one reason why this label has not been applied by any business yet. Furthermore companies need to be already certified according to the EU Eco Audit (EMAS). A product pass showing the history of origin of the textile is attached to make the path of life comprehensible for customers.

Social standards are installed according to the ILO (International Labour Organisation). Environmental sound production process begins already with the prescription to use ecological sound raw materials and recyclable packaging material. A contentious statement is the prohibition of planes for transport. The prohibition of AZO dyes and chlorine bleaching as well as defined limit values for e.g. heavy metals make sure that textiles do not contain contaminants.

GOTS Global organic textile standard
On the International Conference on Organic Textiles 2005 the aim of a global standard for organic textiles was further sketched out to implement it in nearer future. Meanwhile in September 2006 certification bodies will be finished to shift from conventional to global standard.

The aim of GOTS is to set requirements for organic natural textiles throughout the value chain including social criteria. The standards determine guidelines for labelling organic or blended products. They also declare which chemical substances are prohibited while processing and what companies must do in advance for the environment, for example waste water treatment.

Oeko-Tex standard	The most common international label is the Oeko tex standard. Oeko-Tex is valid worldwide and available in different languages. The Austrian research institute ÖTI developed test specifications for proving the contaminant level of textiles, namely the ÖTN 100. In co-operation with the Institute of Hohenstein they established the International Association for the Assessment of Environmentally Friendly Textiles in the beginning of the 1990ies. This association enhanced the first standards to Oeko-Tex 100. Other textiles institutes joined and made the standard more common. Finally in 1995 Oeko-Tex 1000 could be applied. Developed from the two installed standards Oeko-Tex 100 plus was completed in 1999.
Oeko-Tex standard 100	Basically it characterizes textiles and accessories which are verified against contaminants. It only refers to the health concerns of the garment. The production process of textiles is not taken into account. Criteria range from setting of prescriptive values of pesticides, formaldehyde and heavy metals to prohibition of using insalubrious dyestuffs. Among others usage characteristics colour fastness is determined. The limit values vary according to their later use. Thus textiles are classified in four product groups (Class I baby products, class II products with skin contact, class III products without skin contact and class IV decoration material). Each product group has different limit values increasing the closer to skin. If a product is certified, it can employ the label for one year. Thus an annual control of the product is enabled.
Oeko-Tex standard 1000	Standard 1000 checks in terms of environmentally friendliness the production steps forming the final product without proving textiles on their contaminant level. It regards the company's initiatives to reduce the

	environmental impact of the production site. As well as Standard 100 there are clear criteria and limited values for production. Limited values regard air exhaustion in terms of CO, SO2 and NO2 emissions, waste water amount and effluents' composition as well as noise level, energy efficiency and workplace design. Social criteria are also set.
Oeko-Tex standard 100 plus	Assuming that a company is certified by Oeko-Tex standard 1000 and its products certified by Oeko-Tex Standard 100 it can apply for the Oeko-Tex Standard 100 plus
SA 8000	Founded in 1997 by non governmental association, the Council for Economic Priorities, Standard Accountability International 8000 describes social standards for enterprises. SA 8000 controls social minimum requirements in production and certifies factories worldwide.
	Main claims of SA 8000 are among others the prohibition of child work, guarantee of minimum wages and the achievement of a maximum 48 working hours per week including one day off.
	SA 8000 determines social responsibility of employees, suppliers, customers and society. By SA 8000 a differentiation between environmental sound and socially fair produced products and those products which exploit environment and working conditions of people is given.
	Acting socially sustainable by building a worldwide valid certification scheme and a control system for each company. A difference to all other labels is made by questioning employees directly as well as shareholders of outside the company (for example unions).

Labels for certified wood

FSC The international organisation of Forest Stewardship Council was founded in the United States of America in 1990 with the aim to define "responsible and sustainable foresting". Companies of foresting and wood industry, ethnic groups and environmental organisations joined to work out a certification scheme for a global label. Finally in 1993 it could be agreed upon the standards that need to be fulfilled for getting the FSC label.

The vision of FSC is a forest management that is firstly environmentally appropriate, secondly socially beneficial and thirdly economically viable. FSC can be regarded as "the only international valid and for costumers trustful wood label for sustainable and social responsible foresting". FSC label is given by FSC certification bodies to companies which meet ecological and social minimum standards. An inspection of the forest is therefore done. Before gaining the FSC label businesses must apply for the Forest Management Certificate (FM) as well as for the Chain of Custody (COC).

PEFC Programme for the Endorsement of Forest Certification Schemes certification process was initiated in 1998 by forest and timber industry on the consensus of all substantial interest groups with the aim to label wood of economic, ecologic and social sustainable forestry. Its content is based on the decisions made by 37 Nations of the Minister Conference for forest protection. Wood and wooden products which fulfil the PEFC requirements can be signed with the label, if one can secure the Chain of Custody.

Management systems

Environmental management systems — The economic environmental management are according to the Eco Audit Regulation No 1836/93 a part of the overall management system which includes the organizational structure, responsibilities practices, procedures, processes and resources for determining and implementing the environmental policy. In line with economics environmental management systems comprise in broader sense the analysis of the business to its natural environment with regard to environmental polictical and societal aspects.

A differentiation between defensive environmental management which is limited to the legislative measures and proactive management can be made. Proactive management goes beyond legislative environmental measures and enables companies to reduce costs by saving resources, increase sales opportunities in ecologic orientated markets, identify risks, improve conditions for insurance and credit, optimise internal organisation and übernehmen social responsibility for adapting sustainability.

To realize these aims the EU initiated Eco Audit and ISO 14001 are implemented.

EMAS — Eco Audit or Environmental Management and Auditing Scheme is a norm for introduction of an environmental management system in business which is valid in the European Economic Area since 1995. Like other schemes it intends to improve the environmental performance of the organisation in a continuous way.

It claims from companies among others the implementation of environmental guidelines, introduction of environmental protective organisation units and continuous approval of business processes as well as the publishing of an environmental declaration. Participation is based on a volunteer basis and is surveyed by an independent consultant.

ISO 9000   ISO 9000 family deals with quality management standards and guidelines. The known standards ISO 9001, 9002, 9003 have been summarised to the overall standard ISO 9001:2000, which is the latest version.

ISO 9001:2000   Basically ISO 9001:2000 outlines eight basic principles: Customer focus, Leadership, Involvement of people, Process approach , System approach to management, Continual improvement, Factual approach to decision making and mutually beneficial supplier relationships. By implementing improvement and control of processes continuously, results regarding higher quality products or services (at the same time to customer satisfaction) as well as better performing business can be made.

ISO 14000   ISO 14000 is the international norm for environmental management systems in businesses aiming at a continual improvement in the field of the organisations' environmental performance. In difference to EMAS the norm system of ISO derives from a private economic initiative. ISO 14001 as a part of the ISO 14000 family outlines guidelines for introducing the environmental management system, which then gets tested and certified.

OHSAS 18001   The Occupational Health and Safety Assessment Series was designed as an employment protection system by the British Standards Institution (BS 8800) in reference to ISO 9001 and 14001. The system intends to increase motivation of employees by improved work safety and thereby decrease production stops and downtime. It aims at creating competitive advantage as a "safe" company.

Furthermore work safety is an obligatory part for preventing financial miscalculation.

Awards

European Award for the Environment

The Award for the Environment was originated by a European Commission Initiative. Since 1990 this Award is given every two years to one of the nominated businesses to recognise and promote, as an example to others, organisations which make an outstanding contribution to sustainable development. In general the jury for the Award looks at the environmental friendliness and social responsibility within the whole organisation, from management to the production process up to the final product. Criteria that are taken into account are for example emissions, waste and civil protection.

Panda Award

In the sense of WWF three goals, WWF Austria founded the Panda Award on the occasion of the 40th year jubilee in 2003. In the year 2006 WWF could award for the third time special performances in nature- and environmental protection. Awarded get individuals, initiatives and organisations for efforts in environmental protection, which were reached in co-operation with WWF.

Responsible care

Created by the Canadian chemical association in 1984 the certificate Responsible Care describes guidelines for improving the situation for human health-, security- and environment. It was adapted by the European chemical association to implement the programme in national collectives. Conditions to fulfil extend in Austria the legal orders. Two independent examiners put about 200 questions dealing with energy, recycling, employee protection, etc. and judge according to a point system.

The confinement refers to marketing of the award. It may

be applied for company promotion in a period of three years but not for any products. The way of processing and the goals of Responsible Care is similar to EMAS and ISO 14001. The main difference refers to the scope of the award. It also takes business security and protection of employee into account. Of course conditions are adjusted individually to each branch.

Associations and NGOs –labels

Demeter — Demeter is an organisation which goes back to the early 1930ies and the first ideas of ecological farming. During the 20th century the idea of sustainable farming expanded to overseas. In 1997 Demeter consists of 19 independent organisations which form Demeter International e.V. Demeters' best known label is probably the green designed BIO label for biological dynamic food, introduced in market in 2001. Products awarded with the BIO label originate from farms that are certified according to EG-Bio-Regulation (EWG) 91/2092. Meanwhile BIO label can be found in product groups ranging from dairy to frozen products, from beverages and cosmetics to textiles focussing on the whole production process. Cotton and woollen textile materials can be certified, trading companies like Hess Natur utilize the Bio label.

Eco-Tex Consortium — In 1992 Eco –Tex Consortium was established by leading textile and clothing companies to form a network. Four years later it mainly acted as a consulting organisation in terms of quality, safety and environmental friendliness all over the production. By popularising the term "sustainable development" the Consortium focuses meanwhile on installing a global network for sustainable management systems in production areas.

Greenpeace	Greenpeace is environmental organisation with circa 2.8 million members across 40 countries. Since 1971 Greenpeace carries out actions to raise awareness in public towards environmental problems. Most influencing pressurizing medium on decision maker are the spectacular actions, which are non –violant but for actors perilous (e.g. in line with the whale campaign the einsatz of the ship "Rainbow Warrior").
IVN	International Natural Textile Industry Association is a union of companies which have the common aim to produce high quality textiles made under strong ecological and social guidelines. IVN developed two labels for garments made out of natural fibres, Naturtextil and Naturtextil Best. In the value chain, from growing up to finishing health and environmental harmful substances must not be used. Furthermore the two labels claim that certified garments are made under socially fair conditions. Naturtextil Best awards garments which match to all standards whereas Naturtextil awards garments which only partly fulfil the standards.
OTA	The American Organic Trade Association was founded in 1985 and changed to its today's name in 1994. OTA comprises the whole organic industry including non-food in Canada, Mexico and the States. Its mission is "to promote and protect organic trade to benefit the environment, farmers, the public, and the economy". The United States Department of Agriculture (USDA) created with help of OTA the National Organic Program (NOP) which ensures that the used cotton has been grown according to organic agricultural practices with a documentation process throughout the way from farm to bale and thus to finished

garment. If products fulfil the organic standards their labels may contain the word "organic".

PAN Pesticide Action Network was founded in 1982 in Malaysia as a non-governmental and non-profit network with nowadays 600 regional independent organisations. All organisations deal with enlightenment about pesticides, their consequences and possible alternatives. For this purpose PAN tries to influence policy and industry to sharpen legislation wherever pesticides are being used, from organic cotton to domestic gardening, from industrial to less developed countries.

SKAL SKAL is a dutch non-profit organisation founded in 1985 under the name S.E.L. for certification of organic products and their production. According to the EU regulation Number 2092/91 it operates since 1992 as an inspection body for produced, imported or traded organic products. After inspection and successful assessment organic products can be labelled with the black and white EKO sign. Inspection mainly consists of auditing production units like farms and of checking samples of the product.

Soil Association Certification Soil Association was founded in 1946 and started in the 1970ies to develop standards which mostly follow the guidelines of the UK and the European Union. Sometimes the associations' standards are even stricter. SA Certification was established to certify organic food and farming in the United Kingdom. Meanwhile the most important label covers also organic products of other categories. For example it extends to health and beauty products, restaurants and textiles. Textile Certification started in 2003 for natural and animal fibres as well as for leather.

The Global Compact	The GC is an international voluntary initiative launched by the Secretary of the United Nations Kofi Annan in 1999. In spite of the UN governments, companies, labour and civil society organisations joined to turn the vision of a more sustainable global economy into reality. Therefore a guideline was created consisting of ten principles. These principles reach from human rights and labour standards to the environment and anti-corruption area. Any organisation participating in this programme should adapt its philosophy to these principles and try to keep them in everyday life. Due to the fact that the Global Compact has no certification or award status the implementation of the ten principles is not directly controlled. All participators are advised to publish in their annual report or equal corporate reports in which ways they attend and support the initiative.
Members are e.g. Daimler Chrysler and Puma which both integrated the ten principles into their corporate responsibility programme.
WWF	World Wildlife Fund was founded in Switzerland in 1961 by known personalities from economy, science, governments and European royal dynasty. Original WWF aimed at collecting as much money as possible to save threatened animals and plants. Nowadays it is committed to biodiversity and sustainable usage of renewable energy. Financed by almost 5 million people it is the biggest global environmental protection organisation.
Besides the protection of environment WWF is engaged in economy and industry. For example it co–operates with 60 companies (e.g. OBI/Tengelmann, Metro, Pimkie) to develop environmental programmes on a basis of three years minimum to implement long term environmental

strategies. In line with the programme marketing concepts and promotion activities are created. Another programme developed by WWF is The fresh water and cotton initiative where companies like IKEA and Nike joined to develop standard criteria for mainstream companies (established in 2007).